A COLORNI-HIRSCHMAN INTERNATIONAL INSTITUTE 2

The Discovery of the Possible

Excerpts from Political Writings and Correspondence II

EUGENIO COLORNI

THE DISCOVERY OF THE POSSIBLE

Excerpts from Political Writings and Correspondence II

Edited by Luca Meldolesi and Nicoletta Stame
Translated from Italian by Michael Gilmartin

BORDIGHERA PRESS

Library of Congress Control Number: 2019952114

Copyright © 2019, A Colorni-Hirschman International Institute

All rights reserved. Parts of this book may be reprinted only by written permission from the authors, and may not be reproduced for publication in book, magazine, or electronic media of any kind, except in quotations for purposes of literary reviews by critics.

Printed in the United States.

Published by
BORDIGHERA PRESS
John D. Calandra Italian American Institute
25 W. 43rd Street, 17th Floor
New York, NY 10036

A Colorni-Hirschman International Institute 2
ISBN 978-1-59954-159-4

Table of Contents

Introduction: The Topical Politics of Eugenio Colorni, by Luca Meldolesi	11
Postscript	51
Appendix: "Documents on Eugenio Colorni in the Central States Archives"	54

Part I

1. Letter of Agostini to the Directorate of the Italian Socialist Party	67
Anti-fascist Alliances, Tactics, and Political Parties	67
2. The Struggle within Fascism	73
Mass Struggle	74
An Unattainable Position	75
The 1919 Program	75
Illusory Possibility	76
A Political Struggle	77
3. Letter of Anselmi to Joseph	79
Political Function and Organizational Function	79
4. Letter of Anselmi to Joseph	85
Anti-fascist Political and Organizational Activities	85
5. Letter of Ruggeri to Joseph	89
The Problem of the Italian Center	89
Outline of Directives for Italian Work/Activity	94
6. Letter of Ruggeri to Joseph	95
Border Posts	95
Annex: Directives for Establishing Border Posts and for the Work Involved	95
7. Letter of Ruggeri to Joseph	99
Anti-fascist Alliances	99

Part II

1. Letters to Ursula 103
   Systems 103
   Reading Literature 104
   Reading Shakespeare 104
   Reading Kipling, Turgenev, and Slataper 104
   Reading Slataper and Ibsen 105
   Reading Schiller and Shakespeare 105
   Reading Shakespeare and D'Azeglio 106
   Reading Physics and Don Quixote 106
   Two Psychological Mechanisms 107
   Walt Disney, Childhood, and Imagination 108
   Analytic Geometry, Imaginary, and Complex Solutions .. 109
   Popular Poetry 110
   Physical Conditions and Mathematics 111
   Anthropomorphism, Alternative Views, and Animals 112
   Imaginary Numbers and Analytical Geometry 113
   Trieste and Confined Fellows 114
   Jokes and Books 115
   Reading Nietzsche 115
   Mozart and "The Philosophical Illness" 116
   Multiple Undertakings 116
   Birds and "The Philosophical Illness" 116
   "The Philosophical Illness" 117
   Books of Physics and Psychology 117
   Studying Physics 117
   "The Philosophical Illness" and Reading Nietzsche and Thomas Mann 118
   The German Language, Not Submitting to It 119
   Psychology 120
   Dialectics and Great Philosophers 121
   Philosophies and Coherence 123
   Physics, St. Augustin, and St. Thomas 124
   Nervous Diseases Induced by Parents, in Psychology and Literature 125
   Hegel and Dialectical Unrest 126
   Tiredness, Loneliness, and Hard Work 126
   My Few Intelligent Ideas 127
   Hoping in a More Relaxed Work 127
   Reading Huxley 127
   Breathing Your Same Air 128
   Rhetoric of Peasant Life and Paradoxes 128
   Reading Lawrence 129

Authors' Self-indulgence	129
Lawrence's Sons and Lovers	130
Two Types of Novelists	131
Need for Irony in Literature	132
Assimilation of Classics in Our Culture	132
Re-reading Certain Classics	133
Being Victim of a Joke on April Fool's Day	134
Reading Hemingway	135
Living with the 'Soul' of a Writer, Not Becoming One	135
Love as Unstable Equilibrium	136
Being Idle and Natural	137
Will to Live and Feeling Changed	137
Reading Rilke	138
Rilke: Spiritual Creation and Physical Delight	139
Rilke: Love Is Difficult	139
Rilke: Love Helps You Becoming a World	139
Your Ability as a Young Woman Understanding Rilke	140
Down with Style in Literature	141
My Affinity with Reichenbach	141

PART III

1. Ursula Hirschmann, "A Letter of Eugenio's: Melfi 1942"	145
2. Last Wishes of Eugenio Colorni	149
3. Letter to Altiero Spinelli	151
Pantagruelian Attitue, Political "Ideology," and a Future Action for the European Unity	151
4. Letter to Altiero Spinelli	163
Post-war Germany, Collectivism, and Market	163
5. Letter to the Ventotene Federalists	169
Political Situation, Anti-fascist Parties, and Federalist Initiatives	169
6. Letter to Ernesto Rossi	177
The Politics of Federalism as a Movement	177
7. Letter to Federalist Friends in Switzerland	179
Political-military Situation, Political Parties, and Federalist Movement	179

8. Letter-Report to Altiero Spinelli and Ernesto Rossi 187
Report on Action Within the Socialist Party in Rome and on Publishing the Federalist Manifesto 187

9. Report on Federalist Activities to Altiero Spinelli and Ernesto Rossi 191

Bibliography 193

Index of Subjects 197

Index of Names 199

Introduction:
The Topical Politics of Eugenio Colorni[1]

1. "It seems I've been speaking in prose without knowing it!" Eugenio Colorni might have exclaimed (echoing Molière[2]). A political intellectual, Colorni was never at a loss when it came to exuberance and self-irony.

Of course to be able to say such a thing he would have had to know before the fact about Albert Hirschman's theorizing on possibilism[3] (and perhaps even the attribution of this discovery to himself, which is our intention in this note...[4]). And yet, since we live first and think things over later (Geertz), it is not after all so peculiar that such a *post factum* attribution should take place — almost like the posthumous upgrading of some of the previously-ignored canvasses of a great painter.[5] Indeed, as we shall see, the political writings of Eugenio Colorni, assembled here and in the preceding volume,[6] are

---

[1] I thank Mario Quaranta and Nicoletta Stame for their practical assistance in this research; and I thank Florindo Rubbettino for the re-publication in English of texts by Eugenio Colorni published by the Rubbettino Publishing House: 2016, 2017a, 2017b. The titles in italics have been added by the editors.
[2] I refer, of course, to the celebrated exclamation of Monsieur Jourdain in "Le Bourgeois Gentilhomme."
[3] Hirschman 1963 and 1971. (When he enlisted in the US Army in 1942 and became an American citizen, Otto Albert Hirschmann changed his name to Albert Otto Hirschman.)
[4] Cf. Meldolesi 1998. "Colorni," as I wrote later (2004, p. 35), "said that concrete situations consist of relations, relations among people and relations between people and things — they are part of relational society. Eugenio and Albert show us how this often hides peculiarities that are much more vivid and important than they might initially seem. The point is knowing how to intercept them, which often involves coming out of one's shell and going to meet them. This is a theory of knowledge, 'possibilism,' that Eugenio originated and Albert developed. It is a theory of human choice that powerfully expands the ability to enter into and change collective life."
[5] The theme also lends itself to a second consideration. Albert Hirschman, as we shall recall below, was in the habit of speaking of Eugenio in the present tense, as if he had just left the room. Obviously, this does not permit the attribution to him of experiences and events that happened after his death (which would constitute anachronism). But if we proceed with due caution, Albert's habit may allow us, for educational purposes, to use ideas that he developed using Eugenio's work as a starting point, to in turn shed light on Eugenio; and the reverse as well — to explore such ideas in order to bring the thorny problems of today into clearer focus. This is the resourcefulness of possibilism.
[6] Colorni 2019. [Up to now there had been only a "first selection" of Eugenio's political writings edited by Leo Solari (1980, pp. 95 and ff.): "a partial foretaste of a subsequent

dominated by the need to find a way forward (the possibilism of ways out) and to imagine the future (the possibilism of proposals). The reader can verify in person that there is no political text of Colorni's from the thirties and forties that does not have one or the other of these purposes (or both), and which does not arise from the need to admonish, convince and direct the people it is addressed to. And these are precisely the two forms of possibilism later developed by Hirschman,[7] who was at the time — as we shall see below — the acquired relative and, for almost two years, both a participant observer and Eugenio's close collaborator in both thought and deed.

And this is the point. Because it is apparent that the discovery of possibilism is rooted in pain — in the European tragedy of the time and in the immediate and compelling need to contrive a way to fight fascism and Nazism — even though this meant starting from within the contemporary culture, which was heavily burdened with ideological influences, both right and left. It was this profound need for cultural and political liberation that pushed Eugenio (first) and his younger brother-in-law Albert (later) toward a careful, concrete, lucid, naive ("innocent"[8]) observation of reality, aimed precisely at finding ways out and workable proposals. Aimed, in other words, at the discovery and minute exploration of the possibilities among the many existing alternatives — of at least part of the available spectrum of solutions. Ways and proposals that are often new and unexpected and for this reason difficult for many repetitive, guarded and/or narrow mindsets.

With one clarification. Possibilism was discovered by Eugenio and understood by Albert in the 1930s, a time of both talk and ac-

---

initiative" that Solari promised for the future, but which never came to fruition.]

[7] Indeed, my 1994 book (English translation 1995) on his work is entitled, *Discovering the Possible. The Surprising World of Albert Hirschman*; he long explored this world not least because it had already been discovered by Eugenio. The fact that, apart from my own contribution, this correspondence was not even noted by the many commentators in the three volumes marking the centenary of Eugenio's birth (Degl'Innocenti, Cerchiai and Rota, and Zucca, eds.) is probably due to two factors: the scattering of Eugenio's political texts, now being collected, and the unfamiliarity of the critics with the Colorni-Hirschman analytical position which (here and elsewhere) it is my intention to clarify and highlight.

[8] Contrary to the general view, this perspective exalts innocence (Colorni) and naivete when (and to the extent that) it permits a focus on aspects of reality that would otherwise be glossed over. Cf. Colorni 1998, Hirschman 1963, Meldolesi 1998.

tion. But it was then distilled and theorized by Hirschman as a key reference point for his ideas *after* he had decided to devote himself wholeheartedly to intellectual work. This is to say that when the goal is truly to navigate ways out and practical proposals in concrete situations by combining "doing" and "saying," it is essential to learn once again from the political writings of Colorni. This is another important reason, even beyond their historical-political significance, why these texts should finally be collected and published in English.

2. Colorni was first politicized in the revival of progressive ideas that began to show up in Italian universities in the late twenties and found expression in certain "political and cultural journals such as *Rivoluzione liberale, Quarto Stato, Pietre,* etc."[9] linked to Giustizia e Libertà and socialist circles.[10] Having taken a degree in philosophy, Eugenio won the competition for a middle-school teaching post; and, after some initial teaching experience, moved to Germany for professional reasons. Working as a lecturer in Italian at Marburg, he often went to Berlin in 1932–33 to pursue his research on Leibniz at the Staatbibliotek (where he met Ursula and then Albert Hirschmann). He thus helplessly (or nearly)[11] witnessed Hitler's rise and the debacle of Germany's powerful social-democrats. He gave up (with good reason[12]) the idea of an academic career, took a job at the Giosuè Carducci Institute in Trieste, and published Leibniz's Monadologie, with his own long introduction, as part of a series edited by Giovanni Gentile.[13]

During this same period, having put behind him a brief overture to the Giustizia e Libertà movement, which had left him somewhat disillusioned, he decided to join the Socialist Party, appreciat-

---

[9] Merli 1963, p. 13. It is no coincidence, in fact, that the first article by Colorni, then a student of aesthetics, appeared in *Pietre* in 1928.
[10] Of course there is a vast literature on this subject for the reader who seeks more context.
[11] In fact, the tract opposing Hitler written by Ursula and Albert, at the time young social-democrats, was mimeographed in Eugenio's hotel room.
[12] Not least because in the meantime the two professors he had worked with at the University of Milan had been investigated (Martinetti) or de facto self-exiled (Borgese).
[13] Colorni 1934. Gentile had earlier met Eugenio at Forte de Marmi.

ing its anti-fascist position and close rapport with the workers and the masses. He thus decided to involve himself in politics, ideas and action — while at the same continuing his scientific research. He probably realized even then that a challenging political choice of this sort had to be supported by the accompanying development of finely tuned analytical and propositional capabilities by which he could perceive and intercept the infinite nuances of reality. And could thus properly utilize the energy and the economic and political potential that such nuances harbor — what we, with Albert Hirschman, today call "possibilism."

Of course this mental attitude was set (de facto) on a collision course with the ideological-political culture (traditional and/or newly minted) of the Socialist Party, but it represented above all, in the miserable situation of the time, a breath of concreteness, enterprise and youth. It was for this that Colorni was appreciated despite the small earthquake he was about to provoke.

Even though he was only 26, Eugenio did not need to "pay his dues." His first explicitly political text, "Problems of War"[14] was published in August 1935 in *Politica Socialista. Rivista teorica del Socialismo Italiano. Socialismo e Libertà*, printed in Paris and edited by Angelo Tasca. Here he already showed the makings (and acuity) of a leader.

Writing the article, Maurizio Degl'Innocenti tells us, "had been very laborious."[15]

Specifically, we know that Berto (Morandi), then a leading exponent of the internal Socialist Center based in Milan, had asked for a correction with respect to the key role of the middle classes in the antifascist awakening.[16] Faravelli instead appreciated Color-

---

[14] Now in Colorni 2019.
[15] Degl'Innocenti 2010, p. 85. "And it is worth the trouble," he adds, "to reconstruct its antecedents so as to understand the way anti-fascism expressed itself mainly by cultivating a space for the free circulation of ideas [. . .]. The natural outcome of this activity was print publication and distribution. Especially underground, the articles took on a sort of programmatic official status; they were a product of the whole group, even when the responsibility was attributed to a single author. Otherwise an editorial note circumscribed the scope of the discussion."
[16] Ibid., p. 84–87. "Reservations arise," Morandi had written (in Solari, 1980, p. 33, n.), "when Agostini [Colorni] attributes to the middle classes not only priority in the present resistance during the war, but also a sort of initiative in the future revolution, which would take material shape in the development of the more generic anti-authoritarian ideology that will constitute

ni's "more practical" and so "more welcome" position as compared with what their foreign comrades were doing; but he observed that "in a forum where such pressing problems were discussed [such as the war in Abyssinia], publishing a journal every three months is ridiculous!"[17] It was essential, in his view, to turn the article into a pamphlet. Finally, Tasca argued that "the whole first part of Colorni's article is basically a polemical answer to the editorial in the 2nd issue of *Politica Socialista*."[18]

Nevertheless, it was decided to publish Eugenio's paper, also because, as Faravelli observed,[19] "the agreement between the editorial staff and Agostini [that is, Colorni] on how to respond to the Ethiopian war is perfect, and for this reason the Agostini article can be considered the Italian comrades' official position." It then became important to establish *how* to publish the article. In other words, how to do it in such a way that the point of view of this young socialist leader could be supported by the editorial office, while at the same time preventing and blurring the opposition that it might cause in the Party.[20]

The solution was to make some corrections with the consent of the author[21] and to publish it in issue n. 4 of *Politica Socialista* as the

---

the common basis on which all of us will initially agree, [. . .] but as to the effects of the general transformation of society that Agostini himself declares inevitable, [. . .] isn't it clear that starting now it is necessary to establish that our path and the path that the middle classes follow are inevitably divergent?" The truth is that Colorni, as Leo Solari explains (Ibid., p.33), abstained from then on "from indulging in mythologizing the 'working classes,' an obligatory ritual in the catechism of the Socialist and Communist Parties." And that is not all. In my view it should be added that attempts (whether from left or right), stemming from a mistaken need for mental order, to pigeon-hole Eugenio's treatment into an a priori correspondence and/or contrast between the middle and working classes... look worn out—or rather, they say less about the actual merits of the argument than they do about its author. That is to say, they point to a substantial lack of understanding with regard to Eugenio's interpretive point of view and his typical liberating attitude toward a priori blueprints, which we intend to clarify here.

[17] Letter from Joseph [i.e. Faravelli] to a courier for Italy of 1 May 1935, in AA.VV. 1963, p. 133. (Clearly, reasons of space prevent the publication of critical reactions to Colorni's articles and letters, some of which may in any case be found in collections of documents of the period, such as the one just cited).

[18] Letter from Tasca to Faravelli of 4 June 1935, in ibid., p. 142.

[19] Letter from Joseph [Faravelli] to a courier from Italy of 1 May 1935, in ibid., p. 128.

[20] On the other hand (cf., n.15 above), presenting the article as a simple contribution to the discussion would not do if it was to be considered the authoritative opinion of the comrades in Italy, written from within the country.

[21] Cf. Tasca's letter to Faravelli of 4 June 1935, in AA.VV. 1963, p. 142; and Joseph [Fara-

third article — that is, after an editorial entitled "The Abyssinian war and the future of Italy" (which served, among other things, to rectify the editorial in No. 2 and therefore also to implicitly dampen the underlying polemic in the Colorni article that had been picked up by Tasca). And also after a fairly predictable article by Pietro Nenni that moved along well-known pathways (references to Lenin and Rosa Luxemburg, relations between socialists and communists, the question of war and peace, etc.).

And yet, despite the many arguments, corrections, and abridgments, there is no question but that, reading this article of Eugenio's with an ear tuned to possibilism, you feel his spirit begin to assert itself, starting with his concrete observation of the present state of affairs. Take, for example, the following passage[22]: "Already, the Abyssinia mobilization allows us to make interesting observations and offers new opportunities for our struggle. [. . .] First of all, there is a notable absence of enthusiasm, even among volunteers. Enlistment is an entirely calculated way of swapping their present unemployment for a job they hope will be lucrative and not very dangerous [. . .]. They go to war in the spirit of mercenaries. I believe the strongest climate of opposition is to be found among the middle classes, where there is a feeling, more widespread now than ever and confirmed on

---

velli]'s letter to a courier from Italy of 1 May 1935, in ibid., p. 128.

[22]Colorni 2019, p. 21–22. Cf., as well, the previous page of the article, where Colorni describes the "sorcerer's apprentice logic" (you might call it) of Mussolini's foreign policy: "The contradictions it struggles with, the absurdities it faces and the abyss it will fall into," he writes, [. . .] "are intrinsic to any policy that exploits national feeling (vibrant, essential, irrepressible and never to be ignored, but requiring other outlets and forms of expression) as an incentive for increasing the territorial and military power of one nation to the detriment of others." Mussolini, Colorni adds (we are in 1935, don't forget), "now finds that he is forced to ally himself with French democracy against a German fascism that has become intrusive. He finds himself forced in Austria to play off one fascism against another — this great upholder of national values stifling the most serious of the still unresolved national issues in Europe. He finds himself forced — and here the entire Italian press presents a ridiculous if not pitiful example — to conduct an anti-German campaign, professing shock at the very methods of propaganda and repression of which he was the original master, and creating the fable, unfortunately believed even by many of us, that there is an essential conceptual difference between fascism and national-socialism. Actually, one need only glance at the social makeup, economic ties, intellectual references, and tastes and styles of the two movements to be convinced of their essential similarity and to see that the most evident differences are due neither to their basic structure nor the goals they pursue, but to the natural differences, tendencies and emotional reactions of the two peoples."

this occasion, that they are at the mercy of a despotic will over which they have no control. For four days families watched their sons going off, in the wake of a simple postcard call-up, without knowing anything about their destination, without so much as a line in the newspapers. And suddenly there was a sense of panic."

It is concrete observations like this that contribute to the seductive quality of these political writings in which Colorni is, as we have said, progressively discovering possibilism (without knowing it). Exploring them means being drawn into that terrible period and into the theoretical and practical difficulties around which the workers' movement of the time was debated. And yet it was precisely from here, from within this world, this social and political conjuncture that had developed in opposition and by degrees, that this decisive discovery came. We cannot hear its earliest cries without immersing ourselves in the atmosphere of the time, without feeling the suffering and the need for redemption that it brought along with it; and without understanding that it inspired Eugenio to free himself little by little from all undesirable influences, to consciously take up his own full political responsibility in the face of the current concrete situation.[23]

3. Thus stimulated by criticism from the socialist leadership and encouraged by the reception "Problems of War" had received, Colorni then wrote a letter/memo to the Directorate of the PSI (February-March 1936: cf. below) which, on the basis of the variety of agreements and alliances being set up between the various parties (and revealing a certain confusion of ideas), presented a careful analysis and a set of concrete conditions for implementing the many possible alliances in the anti-fascist struggle – "Alliance with any anti-fascist party or group, of whatever stripe or leaning"; "Popular front with the middle classes"; "Socialist and Communist Party action units"; "Organic unity" – whose purpose was to define, little by little, a "real-

---

[23] Leo Solari argues that Eugenio's political writings divide naturally into two groups: articles and letters from the "Internal socialist center" period, and writings from the period of the war and the Resistance — in other words, from before and after his imprisonment and internment. This introduction will follow the same binary division, capitalizing (in part) on Solari's work.

ist" socialist policy[24] that could actually "get things done."

This is a point of view that (in reaction to the noted appeal "to our brothers in black shirts" by the Communist Party) Eugenio returned to in "The Struggle within Fascism," published in the Paris edition of *Nuovo Avanti!* of 31 October 1936: cf. below). Especially at the end of this article we find once again the down-to-earth, possibilist inspiration that interests us here, where Colorni writes that the "position, the only one that can really be adopted on a large scale among the working masses and have any possibility of success is that of propaganda not directed at the fascists, but in the fascist context. Italian workers, almost none of whom are party members, are nevertheless under the influence of fascism, in working men's clubs, in the unions and schools, in sports clubs. This influence doesn't turn them into [fascist] militants, but it makes them people for whom fascism is a fact of life, passively borne, in which they do not always recognize the oppressor directly." We have to present ourselves to them, he adds, "as normal people for whom fascism is, as it is for everyone, the environment, a fact that can only be accepted and to which direct opposition would be madness. We have to make sure young people are educated about the class struggle as something independent, without clashing directly with the regime [. . .] We promote actions to demand things that fascism has never claimed officially to want to deny us."[25]

So it was that, appealing to the desire for justice and action

---

[24]"For Colorni," writes Degl'Innocenti (2010, p. 90), "the central problem was to pave the way for the fall of fascism, which he lucidly declared would result from the joint impact of internal and external factors. With that end in mind he did not rule out any slogan as long as it stirred up discontent toward fascism and the "exploiting classes," and he approved of any action, legal or illegal, that formed a basis for the 'participation of the Italian people in their own revolution.'"

[25]Together with a letter signed 'Maro' (Lucio Luzzatto), Colorni-Agostini's letter was republished by the communist journal *Stato Operaio* in the section "Problems and discussion" with the title "Two letters from socialist comrades in Italy", followed by an editorial comment signed 'r. g.' that finishes with the following words (1937, p. 800): "Finally, Agostini deals with the question of 'propaganda' (why propaganda?) 'not directed at the fascists, but in the fascist context.' We have already stated our case concerning fascists and fascist cadres. We entirely accept, however, the methodological indications that Agostini gives for working in the 'fascist context'. They derive from an understanding of reality that we wish would inspire the Directorate of the P.S.I., which instead seems to treat these problems with a lack of attention that borders on carelessness."

among young people and resourcefully redeveloping — from within Italy — revolutionary positions that had originated with Morandi,[26] Colorni gained prestige within the PSI to the point that (after Rodolfo Morandi's arrest and after the raids of April 1937) he became supervisor of the internal Center.[27]

From this position, Eugenio published, in the 12 June *Nuovo Avanti!*, "Spontaneity as a Form of Organization"[28]: an article which — as may be guessed from the title — was of highly innovative significance with respect to the dictates of tradition.[29] His reasoning is based on the situation in Trieste, which he describes with insight, particularly its favorable political and social aspects, arguing that if the revolutionary parties fail to take advantage of the situation it is because of "certain structural defects" stemming from the intrinsic difficulties of "a certain type of organization."

"The immediacy of people's reaction to recent events," Colorni explains, "and the speed at which news, moods and slogans have spread reveal elementary forms of organization latent in the masses that it would be a very serious mistake to ignore.

Connections — person to person and group to group contacts — exist independently of parties. They are the links of long-standing friendship, kinship or cooperation that every worker has with every other, they are the ties of shared labor, reciprocal trust and everyday

---

[26]Degl'Innocenti 2010, p. 93. Regarding the criticism he received (cf. above, section 2), it is notable that Eugenio had by now acquired the ability (which he would then pass on to Albert Hirschman) to avoid open confrontation and rather to agree to a reformulation that absorbed the positive aspects of his counterpart's position.

[27]As Degl'Innocenti writes (Ibid.), "It was Colorni who wrote a message to the Directorate of the [Socialist] party concerning relations with the communists (and with leftist dissidents) on the eve of the 3rd Party Congress abroad (Paris 26–27 June 1937) [also mentioned in Eugenio's letter to Faravelli-Joseph of 6 August: cf. below]where Faravelli-Lombardi reported on the clandestine work of the Center." In addition, in the summer of 1937 Eugenio was able to obtain directly from the police chief, for "serious family reasons," a passport that allowed him to participate in a philosophy congress in Paris on Descartes that he had been invited to (cf., below, Faravelli-Joseph's letter of 11 August). On that occasion he met the emigré socialist leaders for the first time.

[28]Now in Colorni 2019.

[29]As Leo Solari writes (1980, p. 115), "The text was conceived by Colorni as a contribution to the discussion in anticipation of the meetings that the PSI was preparing to hold in Paris in June 1937." Cf. n. 27.

habit.[30] The spirit of the masses is so homogeneous and widespread that every worker and every bourgeois may be said to have his or her own way of obtaining information, expressing opinions, commenting on facts; they each have, in other words, a personal political environment that feels safe, and that they wouldn't want to trade for other regulated and tested systems. Up to now, these environments have almost always been reserved for ineffectual grumbling and harmless gossip. But they can quite easily (as we have seen in recent months) evolve into more serious shapes. Once a word, a news item, or a pamphlet has been inserted into this network, it moves and spreads by itself, with no need for an additional push, and in no time it is a word or pamphlet that is known to everyone."[31]

This also made it possible to free the few at the top "from direct political contact with many elements at the base, a type of contact through which *agents provocateurs* are known to be easily inserted. The leaders will then be more free to pursue their connections with foreign comrades and their press work, responsibilities involving narrower technical expertise and a number of managers that is limited and not easily known. They will of course need to maintain contact with the masses to keep abreast of their needs and moods and follow their movements. But they can do this innocuously, legally,

---

[30] This situation is quite different from one in which people from different backgrounds meet. In this case, Colorni (2019, p. 28–29) had already explained, "The socialist or communist worker, although extremely concerned with political problems, is today reluctant to take on specific responsibilities which he knows carry great risks and whose effects long experience has made him skeptical about. [. . .] Experience teaches us that the greatest dangers arrive when individuals from different environments come into contact: intellectuals and workers, trustees from the center and individuals from the base, petty bourgeois and proletarians."

[31] "The main risk of newspapers as a propaganda vehicle," he writes shortly thereafter, "is the difficulty of their distribution, which can easily allow the police to piece together the structure of the organization. But when distribution is entrusted to a system that is automatic, so to speak, and separate from the organs of the party, the only problem left is delivery and packaging at the site." According to Bruno Visentini (whom Colorni-Ruggeri had presented to Faravelli-Joseph "for the Brenner frontier": cf., below, the letter of 11 August), "Colorni's project to bring clandestine printed material over the mountains by means of skiers was not followed because as long as it was possible to have a passport it was much easier to bring it by train, in a suitcase, possibly traveling in a sleeper car" (letter to Elio Franzin of 25 October 1965). This in fact was done by, among others, Albert Hirschman, who possessed an impeccable German passport and traveled in an SS officer's uniform, carrying the clandestine printed material — he told me — not in the false bottom of the suitcase, where the authorities would have looked, but in the cover.

without betraying their illegal activities."

Faravelli's letters of 1937, which the reader will find below, in fact argue for unprecedented organizational forms that effectively correspond to these needs — such as a clear separation between, on one hand, the political tasks of a restricted internal Center which is flexible and in direct contact with the foreign Center and, on the other, the organizational tasks of the various local groups, connected through a person provided with a passport to border posts (and ports) directed by the external Center.

4. It is clear that in those years Colorni's life was vibrant and extraordinarily fertile. This was also because the many points of analysis, scattered as we have seen throughout his first political writings, were not in any way improvised — they represent the application (along with the testing and strengthening) of an intellectual point of view that Eugenio himself was at the time fine-tuning.[32]

In fact, not only do the example passages that we have chosen above offer extraordinary glimpses of the reality of the time: they also suggest appropriate tactics for progressing intelligently in undertaking anti-fascist action. The Abyssinian war allowed the unmasking of the pretense of fascist patriotism and brought on board significant sectors of the middle classes; the fight "within the context of fascism" in a certain sense allowed a response that gave the regime a taste of its own medicine[33]; at the same time, organizational work supported the anti-fascist mass struggle and made repressive activity more difficult.

It was a way of thinking and acting that Eugenio also applied to himself — to his rise within the PSI; to his many legal activities in Trieste, which we shall now address; and to his behavior while interned on Ventotene. In all these contexts, in fact, it is possible to

---

[32] A point of view that he would try and make clear in a simple and crystalline form to his wife, Ursula Hirschmann, in his letters from prison and internment (cf., on this subject, Colorni 2019 and below), and about which he would then theorize extensively at Ventonene.
[33] "Just as the fascists used language against us," Eugenio wrote, "that was meant to confuse us and to derail the struggle from the issue of class onto more generic and muddled terrain where they could beat us because we were unprepared, in the same way we have to make use of this vague and uncertain terrain to reintroduce the notion of class as something new."

focus on his typically careful way of analyzing real situations and figuring out how, with full knowledge of the facts, to distill from them ways out and prospects to be pursued.

Thus it was that, alongside the clandestine activities that occupied most of his time, which included helping his wanted comrades escape the country or importing anti-fascist literature from abroad, Eugenio pursued and conscientiously adhered to numerous activities that were completely above board: teaching, theoretical research, and an intense social life — his "cover" — in which he was assisted by his wife Ursula, which included tennis, the opera, intellectual friends, etc.

A guide to understanding the bridge that existed between the two types of activity is a pamphlet of great value that brings together three of Eugenio's articles from *Nuovo Avanti!*, from July-August 1937,[34] concerning, respectively the function of the teacher, of the instruction itself, and of the professor in fascist schools. This is the text that Colorni-Ruggeri refers to in the letter to Faravelli-Joseph of 11 August (cf. below) when he writes: "I do not see any absolute contrast between the legal position and our work as cadres. What I mean, for example, is that in our local pamphlets we incite the workers to stick up for their rights within the unions. I tried to give a practical example of how I see things in the piece on the schools. We will try to promote similar contributions for other social strata (clerks, workers, students, etc)."

In other words, the pamphlet on secondary school instruction is an example (and also a prototype, a model) of the type of policy to be developed within the context of the regime which, as we have seen, Eugenio had proposed the previous year in "The Struggle within Fascism." It was in this pamphlet, then, that the mindset of thought and action that we have identified gradually merged with prolonged experience and reflection.

Colorni writes, for example, that "the fact that in many schools around a third of the students are partially or totally exempt from fees on the basis of merit, gives an indication of the force of will of these young members of the petty bourgeoisie, the agricultural

---

[34] Now in Colorni 2019.

middle class and the proletariat, who see in education their only chance to rise from the poverty of their present state. Now these young people's earnestness and sense of responsibility opens them to a curiosity about life that makes their political education easy and productive."

At the same time, if the teacher, who "has indisputable moral authority over them [. . .] knows how to make use of his daily contact with his pupils so that one way or another he takes part in the things that interest them, if he is able to establish a certain confidence with them, and especially if he allows them the freedom of speech and discussion in the classroom which makes the lessons lively and interesting, if he is careful to free himself of all the musty scholastic and doctrinal rot and to come before his students as a modern man, living in his own time and taking an interest in today's problems; then he will easily succeed at winning their hearts and will gain significant influence over them."[35]

5. This 1937–38 experience in Trieste undoubtedly left its mark on all the participants. Eugenio knew he was being watched, but he skillfully played the role of the philosophy professor passionately immersed in his work — perhaps living with his head in the clouds, but when necessary also in a position to appeal to the authorities.[36]

The balance (however unstable) that he miraculously reached — between family and professional life, teaching and research, legal and clandestine activity — created (among other things) a climate of intellectual effervescence around his life, even in the context of fascism.

Eugenio considered Albert Hirschman (who had taken refuge in Trieste after briefly participating in the Spanish civil war) "my younger brother"[37]; and found time to foster his intellectual meta-

---

[35] Colorni 2019, p. 34–35. I read this essay of Colorni's only recently and I realized that my experience of university teaching in Naples in the eighties and nineties of the last century indeed had some surprising similarities with that of Eugenio in Trieste in the thirties.

[36] Which is exactly what happened in the case of the passport: cf. n. 27. As we shall see, along with his conspiratorial caution (among other things, his continually changing pseudonym: Olanda, Agostini, Anselmi, Ruggeri, D.4, D.5, Commodo, Angelo, Aldo etc.), this attitude would save him twice after his arrest: first enabling him to avoid a heavy prison term, and then facilitating his transfer from the island for family reasons.

[37] "Last Wishes": cf. below.

morphosis, to the point of setting up a sort of family contest with his brother-in-law to discover new ideas in different disciplines.[38]

He also brought together a group of anti-fascist intellectuals imbued with freedom of thought and concrete commitment. In Hirschman's memory there was a further important consequence which, at the time, was for Colorni probably no more than an intuition.

As Hirschman said later,[39] Eugenio "cultivated and relished an intellectual style in which nothing was taken for granted except his own doubts.[40] At the same time, there was one certainty he and his friends were in fact attached to — they were deeply committed in their opposition to the fascist regime. What fascinated me was the fact that a mental orientation free of ideological commitments was intimately bound to a commitment to an extremely dangerous form of political activity. It was precisely in this spirit of experimental cu-

---

[38]Meldolesi 2010. "In contrast to what many economists (and students of economics) generally think even today, Eugenio taught Albert that it was necessary constantly to cast doubt on one's certainties and put them to the test of experience — including the direct and indirect signals we receive daily from reality. He taught him that we need to be receptive, to know how to organize our senses in such a way as to receive and properly process the concrete messages from life and from study, especially those that are unexpected and that perhaps cast doubt on what we think. That we need to fight against our psychological resistance, engaging in a real battle with ourselves to get at even a kernel of truth (with a small t, because the one with the capital T promoted by the philosophers doesn't exist) — of real truth, that is, that goes a bit beyond what we already know. That we need to accept being caught short, being surprised by facts and ideas that prove us wrong (the methodological premise of surprise); and even that we ought to be ashamed of (but not shamed by) what was in our minds before (because, Eugenio explains, the deepest knowledge flows through us, sets us in motion — it is something that we do not easily forget . . .)." (Meldolesi 2013, pp. 68–69. Hirschman dedicated a famous monograph (later included in the 100 most important social science essays of the second half of the 20th century) — *Exit, Voice, and Loyalty* (1970) — "to Eugenio Colorni (1909–1944), who taught me about small ideas and how they may grow."

[39]Hirschman 1987; now in 1990, p. xxxi.

[40]Eugenio thus suggests that cultivating doubts and misgivings can prove fruitful. "Indeed, the world we live in is far more complex than current thinking allows for — a doubtful and vigilant attitude may be the first step toward reaching more valid and discriminating convictions that make a person stronger rather than weaker. It thus happens, by a process that is only at first sight paradoxical, that it is (consciously formed) doubts rather than (often presumptive) certainties that motivate action. This is the opposite of the proud and intransigent attitude that, like a dialog between deaf people, prevails among philosophers and elsewhere." As Hirschman later added, "It is a mental inclination that shows the willingness of the subject to form his or her own beliefs on the basis of experience, factual data, and the opinions of others: a key ingredient in the successful functioning of the deliberative processes of our democracies" (Meldolesi 1998, p. 26).

riosity that Colorni and his friends faced the philosophical, psychological and social questions that spurred them into action in situations in which freedom of thought was under attack or in which the injustice was obvious and the stupidity intolerable. It was as if they had set out to prove that Hamlet was wrong — as if they wanted to show that doubt could *motivate* action instead of weakening or discouraging it. Moreover, they did not consider their participation in highly risky political activities as the price to be paid for their freedom of thought, but rather as a simple, natural, spontaneous and almost lighthearted *quid pro quo*. Their attitude has always seemed admirable to me as a way of looking at political activity and of combining public and private life."

This is a key bit of reasoning that we must not allow to slip away.[41] "If I had time," Albert concluded, "I could explain that we all can still learn from this example. Indeed, this type of coexistence of a commitment to public life with great intellectual openness seems to me the ideal micro-foundation of an effectively democratic society."[42]

This is obviously a posthumous assessment, written while Albert was working on his *Rhetoric of Reaction*[43] (reaction from the right, but also from the left). To fully appreciate its meaning we have to jump back in time, with these ideas in mind, over an entire historical era and all it has taught us (explicitly and implicitly).

And yet, in the light of what has been written up to now, it seems to me that Hirschman's observations already contain an extraordinary appreciation of the work of Colorni and his friends. Because despite being conceived under conditions (cultural, ideological, social, political) that were anything but favorable, their critical efforts and attempts to prefigure an alternative to fascism had carried them

---

[41] Some time ago, I used it as the end point for a review of Albert's texts on democracy: cf. Chapter 8 of my *Discovering the Possible: The Surprising World of Albert O. Hirschman* (1994) — a text he liked, because, he told me, it reflects the psychological tension involved in facing the future.

[42] In contrast to the original version in Italian (Hirschman 1987, now in 1990, page xxxi), the English version (Hirschman 1995, p. 119) speaks of "the ideal micro-foundation of a democratic politics." I stick here to the initial text, while also taking into account this second version. (For the revival of this Colornian logic during the Roman Resistance, see below, n. 63.)

[43] Hirschman 1991.

to the point of establishing the ideal micro-foundation for a politics and a society that were effectively democratic. Note that contrary to what an expert reader of things Hirschmanian might expect, Albert does not speak here of "*an*" ideal, but of "*the ideal micro-foundation*"; which is to say, of that set of salient aspects of human behavior that form the basis of the effectively democratic politics and society of the future.

6. But suddenly, Mussolini's race laws, Eugenio's arrest, and the disgraceful antisemitic uproar orchestrated in the press clouded the horizon. Colorni defended himself with great intelligence, pointing to his integrity as a teacher and his passion for his educational and scientific work. He served a six-month sentence in the prisons of Trieste and Varese. Because the police lacked "hard evidence" and the authorities did not want to expose (and thus burn) the informants against him (in Italy and abroad), he managed to avoid the Special Tribunal and consequently a sentence of dozens of years (if not death). He was instead interned on the island of Ventotene, where he arrived at the beginning of 1939.

Thus began one of the most difficult periods of his life. Psychologically, Eugenio felt distant from the other internees and their diatribes. His intention was to remain faithful to the official image of himself as the pure, reserved intellectual that he had displayed to the authorities,[44] not least in order to begin bombarding them with requests: to gradually loosen the bonds of his internment with a view of returning to the mainland.[45] Thus he focused his attention on writing and study (including his truly "heroic" effort to learn several natural sciences as an autodidact); but at times the isolation and psychological fatigue brought on painful crises of depression.

Nevertheless, his extraordinary strength of character allowed him to progress, in successive bursts of intense effort — he studied mathematics, physics and psychoanalysis, digging deep within him-

---

[44]"The internee," in the words of his immediate supervisor (cit. in Tedesco 2014, p. 127), "has given no evidence resulting in any findings concerning his political conduct and has dedicated himself exclusively to study."

[45]To understand the logic and the unfolding of this struggle, see below the following Appendix.

self and producing extraordinary texts. Moreover, his legal battle with the authorities obtained some first results with the reunification of the family (Ursula and little Silvia) at Ventotene.[46]

Then something unexpected happened: Altiero Spinelli (in July) and Ernesto Rossi (in October) were also interned on Ventotene. Ernesto, who was in contact with Luigi Einaudi (and had read texts on English federalism), began supporting the idea of a United States of Europe. Altiero, who had already begun to move in this direction on his own,[47] saw Ernesto's proposal as "a revelation," as well as an extraordinary opportunity to resume his political commitment in a new guise. They spoke about it with Eugenio Colorni[48] and his wife Ursula. In this way, an inseparable quartet was formed at Ventotene (which at the same time fully respected each member's personal inclinations).

Ernesto, of the liberal (later radical) school, was mainly concerned with economics and society; Altiero, a charismatic ex-communist leader, gave vent to his political passion with the federalist idea; Eugenio, the socialist-federalist, continued pursuing his own intellectual and personal development[49]; Ursula, the only one who

---

[46]But perhaps, I would suggest, Colorni did not realize that the total intellectual concentration that allowed him gradually to distill his thinking at the same time caused him to lose touch with the feelings of his wife Ursula, who later became sentimentally linked with Altiero Spinelli, and Eugenio with Luisa Villani.

[47]"During the first half of 1939," Altero remembered (1985, pp. 201–02), "reading not only the articles Einaudi had published in the *Corriere della Sera* at the end of 1918 against the League of Nations and in favor of a European federation, but also several essays by English federalist authors and the book *Nationalstaat und Staatsräson* by Meinecke, [. . .] and meditating on the obvious march of Europe toward another world war — all this made me realize that the future of Europe, once fascism and Nazism had fallen, should probably be sought not in the simple restoration of national democracies, but in the founding of a European federation. [. . .] This idea originated in discussions between myself and Rossi [. . .]. When we began to speak of it with others, Eugenio Colorni and his wife Ursula were among the first to welcome it."

[48]"My way of thinking," Spinelli wrote (1984, p. 300), "would not be what it is if I hadn't had those two years, from my arrival at Ventotene in July of '39 till his departure for Melfi in October of '41, of almost daily dialog — tearing down, examining and rebuilding — with him.": Eugenio Colorni.

[49]At the same time, Eugenio felt the need to rein in the political-moral drive of Altiero. "When I was an adolescent," he wrote in the dialogue "Sull'azione" [On action] (2009, p. 344), "I had three older cousins [Enrico, Enzo and Emilio Sereni], who made it their task to remind me at every turn how far I was from the ideal of virtue and morality that they perfectly represented. I feel now as if I've returned to that time; only there is just

was not actually "interned," made intelligent use of the opportunity to nurture (more easily than the others) her political relations with friends and family on the mainland (while the family grew with the birth of Renata and Eva). Together, they began discussing a great variety of topics and shaping them into dialogues.[50]

The key point of this famous Ventotene "federalist meeting" is that the different political and cultural choices of the four protagonists were initially held in check by a general hypothesis that transcended them. The proposition of a United States of Europe was indeed supported by the expectation that with the defeat of the Axis, the real possibility of bringing about such an eventuality would materialize in the short term, before the old nationalist and imperialist states could get back on their feet.

This conjecture basically rested on two main pillars. In the first place, at the end of the First World War it had happened that the victorious countries had not intervened directly in the reconstruction of those that had been defeated. If analogous conditions prevailed, the reasoning went, it would be possible to build a new institutional structure in Europe, perhaps by means of revolution, that would start in the vanquished countries — primarily, that is, in Germany and Italy.

Moreover, it was at the time believed that, through the effect of a Hegelian historical trick, Hitler's military successes in the first phase of the war would in any case uproot the old European nationalist-imperialist structure, making its eventual post-war reconstruction much less manageable and/or plausible.[51] This meant preparing to

---

one cousin now [Altiero], but doing the work of three. And with this difference as well: at that time I felt guilty all the time and took my cousins' admonitions very seriously; now I couldn't care less."

[50]Now in Colorni and Spinelli 2018.

[51]In this regard, I found it interesting to read the article "Riorganizzazione economica europea" [European Economic Reorganization] by Raffaello Riccardi, Minister for Trade and Currencies under the fascist government (*Antieuropa*, September-October 1940) which discusses the "future direction of the economy," "European autocracy," the "sunset of gold," and "the basic work of money": a text that Edmondo Paolini (1996, pp. 211–15) re-published as "an effective counterpoint, chronological and systematic even, to the federalist line of the *Manifesto* that Spinelli, Rossi, Colorni and a small group of internees were developing at Ventotene: fascism was also worried about the future of Europe after the war, which they thought they would win."

act immediately at the end of the war to trigger the desired change.[52] It was in this political and cultural climate in the spring of 1941 that Altiero and Ernesto wrote the Ventotene Manifesto — or more precisely, *Per un'Europa libera e unita. Progetto d'un Manifesto*.[53]

7. But the famous *Manifesto* was "the result of a wide-ranging debate that went on for several months, with Eugenio Colorni and his wife Ursula Hirschmann and the participation of a small group of internees."[54] The first draft was completed in June 1941; the second (which took into account recent observations and developments in the international political situation, not least the German invasion of Russia) is from August of the same year.[55]

---

[52] "Two years ago," Eugenio wrote to Altiero in May 1943 (cf. below), "when we were thinking about the unity of Europe, it presented itself as a goal to be reached in a single leap, in the period immediately after the cessation of hostilities. 'It is essential,' we said, 'that we not wait for the hot lava to re-solidify in the old molds. We need to strike while the iron is hot, and see to it that when the victors sit down at the peace conference table to give Europe a new orientation, they find before them a Europe already launched on the road to unification by the revolutionary strength of its people. If we can't seize this chance at the opportune moment, we will have lost it forever; and the unification of Europe will have to be put off until the end of the Third World War.'"

[53] "Concerning the *Manifesto*," Altiero later recalled (1984, p. 311), "I wrote the chapters about the crisis of European civilization, the unity of Europe as a permanent postwar task and the necessity of a 'revolutionary party' to bring this about. Ernesto Rossi wrote the chapter on the social reforms to be tackled after the war. But we discussed every paragraph, and I can still recognize the trains of thought of one of the two of us in the parts written by the other."

[54] Paolini 1996, p. 217. According to Altiero's diary, the group was composed of Dino Roberto, Enrico Giussani, Giorgio Braccialarghe and Arturo Buleghin. Graglia (2010, p. 227) states that two Albanians, Lazar Fundo and Stavo Skendi, should also be included. The *Manifesto*, first circulated in the form of a mimeograph, was published secretly in Milan on 29 August 1943 at the conclusion of the constituent convention of the European Federalist Movement; and in Rome (together with two essays by Altiero of 1941- 42) in January 1944, edited by Eugenio Colorni."

[55] "But it is not entirely correct to say," observes Piero Graglia with a touch of irony (2010, p. 15) "as some authors have, that federalist thinking is based entirely on the theorizing of the two authors of the Ventotene *Manifesto* — that is, Rossi and Spinelli enshrined in some reliquary; if a religious concept is really called for it should be the trinity, and the holy spirit in this context is Eugenio Colorni, who took part in the preparatory discussions for the *Manifesto* along with a few others and played a prominent role, especially in stimulating and criticizing the two authors of the document from the standpoint of an independent socialist." In addition, Fabio Zucca (2010, p. 257) writes that "the *Manifesto* was a product of the collective work and daily debate among the three friends [Altiero, Ernesto and Eugenio] with an attentive consultant in Ursula Hirschmann, despite the fact that, as is well known, it was materially written by Spinelli and Rossi."

And yet, after barely two years the basic hypothesis of the *Manifesto* appeared to be obsolete. Indeed, as Eugenio wrote to Altiero (cf. below, his letter of May 1943) "You started out assuming that at the end of the war the floodgates are suddenly going to open and the waters will rush down and submerge everything. And you assigned to yourself and whoever follows you the task of digging the great channel that will guide these waters and make them once again beneficial and fertile. In effect, this is what happened in many European countries in 1918. Will it happen again this time? [...] I don't believe the possibility has ever occurred to you that things might not go this way. Because of a certain mental inertia that always makes us picture things in a a way that will favor the fulfillment of our own prospects, you keep imagining situations in which the unleashed and disoriented masses are looking for a guide, a beacon that will light their way. And you correctly propose that you will be such a guide for them — with greater intelligence and impartiality, with greater attention and attachment to the concrete situation and the needs of the moment than the traditional parties are capable of.[56] But what if things don't go this way? What if tomorrow's postwar period doesn't present this fluid and chaotic aspect, this new primordial state where victory is there to be seized by whoever has the most open mind and the stoutest heart?"

The first objection, then, is that Altiero doesn't examine possible alternatives; he does not take into account the range of practical possibilities. To this, Eugenio adds a second objection, which is that Altiero lets himself fall into "a very common sin [...] which I would call 'ideology'. I have recently had occasion to observe this first hand in people who had made politics the only reason for their existence. They had the same defects and shortcomings that we have so often criticized and laughed at in philosophers. They too built themselves beautiful palaces where they put everything they required, all their 'needs', all their 'ideals of civilization.'[57] For them too, the main wor-

---

[56]This is the political attitude that Eugenio later qualifies as "Pantagruelian": cf. n. 59.

[57]The reader of Colorni's key texts will recognize here one of his main warhorses — as in "Apologo su quattro modi di filosofare" [Apologia on four ways of doing philosophy], which Eugenio had in fact written at Ventotene (Colorni 2009, pp. 188 et. seq.).

ry was whether the palace would stand up in its logical coherence, in its 'circularity'. A political ideology and a philosophical system are in this sense like two peas in a pod. [...] Politics, in my view, will not move forward by retouching its ideological structure [...], but by keeping its eye on developing events and trying to influence them using the most effective and unbiased methods; always, of course, in the light of some basic positions which it should be enough to have clear in one's heart and, I would say, in one's instincts."[58]

All this does not mean that Eugenio underestimated Altiero's notable political qualities (starting with his attitude which, here again, he calls "Pantagruelian"); it is just that in his view, such characteristics ought to have evolved into a vision that was more aware and useful.[59]

And it is precisely to that end that he again displays the pedagogical attitude toward Altiero that he had wielded with success at Ventotene.[60]

8. Eugenio was a political intellectual, Altiero an intellectual politician. This might appear to be an unimportant quibble, but such is not the case. At Ventotene their roles had already been different. Now their diverging points of view revealed the underlying differ-

---

[58] Thus, according to Eugenio, Altiero does not really consider postwar alternatives and does not keep his eye on developing events so as to understand their potential and fine-tune his intervention. In both cases, what was absent was the "possibilism concerning the way out" that we have discussed.

[59] "It is precisely your horror at a situation that is not "Pantagruelian," Eugenio writes, "[...] that sometimes makes your words sound empty and tired. You have planted yourself in the middle of the current, you've built your embankment, and now you're surprised that so little water is swirling past it. You get irritated, exasperated: 'Quit your fussing, roll up your sleeves and get to work.' But the fact is that there where you have planted yourself there is hardly any water. The waters are rapidly opening channels further down, along other banks." To be more precise, Eugenio's rebuke concerns Altiero's 'fever for action,' "which leads you to imagine that you are always in a central position, when in fact your position is peripheral. It's not that your 'Pantagruelian' way is disagreeable or unbearable, or that it offends my sense of freedom and independence. On the contrary, I like it very much and it doesn't offend me at all. But it makes you fall into errors of perspective and make blunders — that's all."

[60] Cf. above, n. 48. So that in his answer Altiero initially wrote, "My dear E., I thank you for your friendly personal criticism. I take it very much to heart, as you well know." Then, however... he let himself off the hook with a joke: "but being unable to discuss it comfortably here, I'll have to put it off until my days of leisure in the second half of the century" (Spinelli 1993, p. 203, n. 8).

ence of position. Eugenio offered possibilist conjectures that were exposed to daily questioning in order to push the group's thinking into the closest possible correspondence with factual reality — a procedure that in itself takes account of the possibility that the initial hypothesis may (entirely or in part) prove to be erroneous. Altiero's attitude was instead more static. He was a politician who constructed his "line" ideologically, starting from certain basic assumptions, so that adapting to an evolving reality sometimes entailed scrapping a position or even changing the "line" altogether.

"The victorious nations of the last war," Eugenio explained later in the letter, "tried to dominate the defeated states through territorial mutilation, military restrictions, economic and financial burdens. But they were not remotely concerned with influencing domestic politics. Germany, Austria, Turkey, Greece, and Italy were left in the grip of their own internal upheavals, 'free', as it was put at the time, 'to choose the regime they thought suitable'. [. . .] Now I don't know how the winners will treat the losers at the end of this war. But one thing I do know for sure — this time they will not make the mistake of staying out of domestic politics. Intentions are very clear on this point, and not a day passes when these are not reaffirmed by all parties involved. They want to depose fascist regimes once and for all and will not allow the resurgence of nationalism, chauvinism, etc. [. . .] This time we are in the presence of two very powerful state organizations that present themselves as paladins of the two basic ideologies contending for the European field. Fighting for one of these ideologies will mean, not only implicitly but in the general consciousness of the people, fighting in favor of the corresponding power. The communism-democracy antithesis has gradually transformed itself into a Russia-England antithesis."

Obviously, no one in this debate was yet able even to *imagine* the dominant role that the United States would have in the second post-war period. In any case, the lines had been drawn: "Russia or England. In these terms, secure in their instincts, the people will interpret every political speech they hear"; and even the two friends, while agreeing about many things,[61] were on this issue at pains to

---

[61] As Altiero in fact answered in June 1943 (1993, p. 203), "I was pleased with the way

pursue the idea of European unity with reference respectively to one or the other of the two sides.[62]

These two attitudes thus coexisted in a transverse Federalist Movement crosscutting a political system that was in the meantime rebuilding itself. The mutual friendship and legitimacy within the two camps was never questioned (which is in itself extraordinary); they evolved and progressed in parallel. Eugenio (who, as we have seen, had managed to get transferred to the mainland for family reasons and had then gone underground to avoid re-internment and to commit himself fully, as a socialist, to the Roman Resistance) even became *pro tempore* leader of the Movement.[63] He also worked on socialist federalism,[64] and after the fall of Mussolini he wrote "Unanimità," an extraordinary editorial for *L'Unità Europea*.[65] In a letter to Ernesto Rossi of 5 August (cf. below) he set out some themes for the founding Congress of the European Federalist Movement at Mi-

---

your letter showed me that developing events have brought our viewpoints closer together," although they nevertheless remained far apart. "Our illusions about England," Altiero belatedly recognized, referring to himself and Ernesto (Spinelli 1984, p. 317), "were slightly inferior to Colorni's about Russia. Strangely enough, the United States, whose constitutional structure had seemed so important to us that we had been ready to propose it as a model for Europe, didn't break into our Eurocentric vision except as little more than an appendage of England."

[62]Daniele Pasquinucci has observed (2010, p. 297) that Colorni was a "political leader with much greater responsibility than the two authors of the *Manifesto*, 'at once a critic and a linchpin' [within the Socialist Party], as Giuliano Vassalli remembered him," with a gift for both "balance and foresight." And I should add that anyone, even a professional historian, who is surprised that Eugenio was trying at the time to imagine a revolutionary solution centered on Germany and the USSR, in my opinion comes close to anachronism — does not, that is, take account of the conditions of the workers' movement of the time (adopting, you might say, a vision that is ex-post probabilist rather than ex-ante possibilist).

[63]"I hope," he wrote in an information letter for the Ventotene federalists in July 1943 (cf. below), "to discharge my function to everyone's satisfaction. Our last discussions had caused me to fear that our shortcomings were too serious to allow us collaborate productively. But the articles you have sent [. . .] clearly show that you also think the tone of the newspaper [*L'Unità Europea*] should be such that both our points of view are entitled to citizenship." (And the exchange of letters of May-June 1943 mentioned above which was prepared — in part — for publication under the title *The Practical Implementation of European Unity: A Discussion Among Federalists*, but was in the end not published: cf. Spinelli 1993, p. 190, p. 3.)

[64]Cf., in Colorni 2019, the statement of principle "The Socialists and the European Federation," published (later) in *L'Unità Europea*.

[65]Colorni 2019.

lan, in which he took an active part,[66] and he wrote a letter/report of great interest on the Roman situation to his federalist friends in Switzerland (where, after their internment had ended, Ernesto, Altiero, and others had taken refuge, accompanied by Ursula).[67] Finally, in January 1944, he published a "booklet" — under the title *Problemi della federazione europea* — which included the Ventotene *Manifesto* and two contemporary essays by Altiero,[68] along with a preface by Eugenio which is a small masterpiece of its kind.[69]

9. The version Colorni edited, which has been printed and reprinted numerous times, is generally considered to be the key text of the Ventotene *Manifesto*, the endpoint of the group's collective work. Edmondo Paolini has pointed out a number of differences with respect to the Milanese version that preceded it — stylistic and structural as well as textual.[70] Clearly, this was a careful editing job

---

[66] Daniele Pasquinucci writes (2010, pp. 283–84) that Colorni "had an important role even in the definition of the strategy and organization of the association, and [. . .] defended — successfully — the idea set out in the 1941 *Manifesto* that the federalists should structure themselves not as a party but strictly as a movement."

[67] Cf., below, the "Letter to Federalist Friends in Switzerland" (November 1943). Referring to the political/military situation in Rome, Eugenio wrote that the "political parties are able to act with a certain facility, in spite of the difficulties and dangers. There is in any case vastly more political life than there was under fascism, even very recently. And there is a combative atmosphere that leads people to confront the dangers with relative cheerfulness. The underground newspapers are buzzing, the streets are full of anti-German and anti-fascist graffiti that the police are unable to erase completely, and each of us has a constant sense of solidarity from the entire population."

[68] "Politica marxista e politica federalista" [Marxist politics and federalist politics] and "Gli Stati Uniti d'Europa e le tendenze politiche odierne" [The United States of Europe and today's political trends]. "The collection of federalist writings edited by Colorni," stated Piero Graglia (1993, p. 34), "was one of the most 'successful' underground publications in Italy." "The 'booklet,'" as Colorni himself referred to it in a letter to Spinelli and Rossi [of 10 May 1944], "had gathered a 'notable consensus,' especially in the Action Party and among the Social Christians, 'those who pursue the construction of a socialist ideology free of the myths of Marxism.' The socialist leaders, on the other hand, viewed the text 'with suspicion, as they would an adversary's book, but it was read with great interest by young people'" (Pasquinucci, 2010, p. 279).

[69] Cf. Colorni 2019.

[70] "Colorni modified the original structure of the document," Paolini writes, "reducing it to only three chapters by moving the first part of chapter IV, 'The revolutionary situation: old and new trends,' into chapter II 'Postwar tasks — European unity'; at the same time, the second part of chapter IV was moved to the end of chapter III, 'Postwar tasks — Social reform.' Along with improving the style, Colorni makes small cuts, especially in the phrases referring to communist politics in Russia and the concordat between Italy and the Holy See."

by Eugenio, who also wrote (almost apologetically) in a letter/report to Spinelli and Rossi of 13 February 1944, "I had to do the preface myself because we couldn't get a copy of the *Manifesto* that you published in Milan."

Colorni's "fine tuning" was welcomed by the two authors[71]; and then by the European Federalist Movement as a whole — to the extent that it became de facto the official version of the *Manifesto*.[72] It is a publication that we must now examine in an unusual way — not so much with reference to itself, that is, as to the conditions and problems of the time *through the political and theoretical eyes of Eugenio Colorni* (rather than those of Altiero, Ernesto, or the Italian federalist tradition).[73]

Seen from this angle it becomes clear, in my view, that there were a number of reasons that motivated Eugenio to commit himself so completely to the editing of the *Manifesto*. It is likely, in fact, that as a way of combating possible disorientation in the face of the evolving situation (mentioned above), Colorni meant the federalist *Manifesto* (by now a historical text, more readable and contemporary thanks to his alterations) to be an anchor for the daily research of the anti-fascists concerning "the situation and our task" (in the language of the time).

In addition, Eugenio considered the Ventotene political chapter in which he had been a protagonist to be an important discovery in political thinking — indeed, probably the most important of the time and capable of producing results (immediate and negotiated, direct

---

[71]According to Mario Albertini (1985, p. 14), Altiero Spinelli explicitly stated that the edition of the *Manifesto* edited by Eugenio Colorni "constitutes the 'authentic and exact text.'" On Eugenio's death in 1944, moreover, Ernesto Rossi declared (now in 1975, pp. 189–92) that "In his few days [of clandestine life, Eugenio had] managed to get *L'Unità Europea* published, put together the first federalist group in Rome, distribute mimeographs of the writings we had sent from Ventotene, and re-establish relations with our friends at various border posts and cities of Italy. [. . .] He was an agitator, a journalist, a dynamiter, a leader of armed bands, and finally he sacrificed his own life. This contrast — the contrast between Eugenio Colorni the intellectual and the political activist that a deep moral need had led him to become — makes his heroic life stand out all the more."

[72]Now part of *Il progetto europeo* by Altiero Spinelli, 1985.

[73]In doing so, I adopt the point of view of the history of political thought and the history of culture respectively developed in the seventies of the last century by Quentin Skinner and Wolf Lepenies in the context of the School of Social Science of the Institute for Advanced Study at Princeton, NJ, then directed by Clifford Geertz and Albert Hirschman.

and indirect) of great importance. In actual practice, protecting and disseminating it meant promoting the birth of a new political vision that was concrete and capable of re-balancing the relationship (in terms of both thought and action) between the worlds inside and outside the country in favor of the latter — a general change of outlook with respect to what had been typical under the old politics.

Moreover, considering the differences of opinion that had already manifested themselves regarding factual reality, the publication and dissemination of the *Manifesto* was also a way of preserving the unity and pluralism of the Federalist Movement, as well as supporting the legitimacy of the socialist component within it.

And finally, of course, if we take into account Eugenio's numerous activities in the Roman Resistance (of which, more below), it becomes immediately clear that the publication of the *Manifesto* in January 1944 was a key element in the extraordinary political initiative he was pursuing at the time.[74]

10. Turning then to Eugenio's preface to the Ventotene *Manifesto* with these concerns in mind, we can perhaps capture its lasting meaning — which reveals itself both in the message that comes down from that time and the needs of the present.

The *Manifesto* sprang from reflections, individual and collective (of a small group) and based on limited knowledge, which took place under conditions that were undeniably grim but which, with respect to the task at hand, nevertheless proved to be (paradoxically) favorable. Indeed, "the isolation from concrete political activity allowed for a more detached view and suggested a review of traditional positions and a search for the reasons for past failures, not so much in technical errors of parliamentary or revolutionary tactics,[75] or in a generic 'immaturity' of the situation,[76] as in deficiencies in

---

[74]In an earlier version, sections 10–13 and the postscript that follows were previewed in Dossier n. 1 at www.colornihirschman.org — site of "A Colorni-Hirschman International Institute," spring 2015.

[75]Here Eugenio in all probability alludes to the endless quarrels between reformists and revolutionaries that had characterized the workers' movement since its inception.

[76]This (probably) derives from the theory of Karl Marx, who argued for the inevitability of social transformation once a certain threshold of capitalist development had been reached.

the general approach and in having committed the struggle to following the usual fault lines, paying too little attention to what was new and was altering the situation."

This secluded position, this "detached view" thus allowed a re-orientation of the action using a novel formulation suggested by the new conditions that were emerging rather than by a critique of the thinking that had been handed down — not that this was excluded[77] (see below).

Indeed, Colorni adds that at Ventotene, "in preparation for efficiently fighting the great battle for the near future that was looming, we felt a need not simply to correct the errors of the past, but to reformulate the terms of the political issues with minds unencumbered by doctrinaire preconceptions or party myths."

"Thus it was," he continues, "that in the minds of certain people the key idea took shape that the basic contradiction responsible for the crises, wars, misery and exploitation afflicting our society was the existence of sovereign states that are geographically, economically and militarily defined, which view other states as competitors and potential enemies, and live in a perpetual state of *bellum omnium contra omnes* with respect to each other. There are many reasons why this idea, although not new in itself,[78] took on a new significance on the occasion and under the conditions in which it was conceived [that is, at Ventotene at the beginning of the 1940s]: [. . .] First of all, the internationalist solution, which appears on the agendas of all progressive political parties, is in a certain sense considered by each of them to be a necessary and almost automatic consequence of achieving the ends that each of these parties proposes."[79]

---

[77]And could not have been, given Eugenio's critical view of Marxist theory.

[78]Think only of the centuries-old rivalries that kept the countries of Europe apart; think of the so-called age of imperialism (and its related literature). The consequences deriving from it, however, were unpublished — before the *Manifesto*.

[79]"The democrats maintain that the establishment within each country of the regime they advocate will surely lead to the formation of that unitary consciousness which, passing beyond all cultural and moral frontiers, will constitute the basis, for them indispensable, of a free union of peoples, even in the areas of politics and economics. And the socialists, for their part, think that the establishment of the dictatorship of the proletariat in the various states will in itself lead to an international collectivist state." Today, fortunately, this rather doctrinaire duality between democrats and socialists no longer dogs us. But this change "for the better" is still of interest — it helps us understand both the road that has been trav-

Eugenio does not venture into their ways of thinking, nor does he deal with the various ideological roots they come from. For him it is enough to show how things actually are, through a simple phenomenological accounting.[80] As he puts it, "an analysis of the modern concept of the state and the interests and feelings linked to it[81] clearly shows that although similarities in internal regimes can facilitate friendly relations and collaboration between one state and another, it is by no means certain that this will automatically or even progressively lead to unification, as long as there are collective interests and feelings associated with maintaining a unity confined within borders."

11. Plainly, Colorni does not deny that a certain internal institutional set-up can have positive effects at the international level. He maintains, however, that this is not guaranteed, and that it is not "a one-way street" — that is, that a given economic-political domestic arrangement does not necessarily determine the international framework.

"We know from experience," he continues, "that chauvinistic feelings and protectionist interests can easily lead to clash and competition even between two democracies; there is nothing to say that a rich socialist state would necessarily pool its own resources with another much poorer socialist state merely because it was governed by a similar regime. The abolition of political and economic borders between states, therefore, does not necessarily derive from the simultaneous establishment of a given internal regime in each state; it is an issue in its own right, and must be tackled using appropriate means

---

eled, and (especially) the limitations of the time (which remain to be discussed) regarding the idea of democracy and its federalist destination.

[80]He seeks the reader's empathy on this point, appealing to common perceptions and common sense. This is an analytical choice that brings to mind that of Albert Hirschman almost half a century later when, rather than following the ultraliberal critics into the rabbit hole of deep reasoning of their reactionary mindset, he pursues an unprecedented phenomenological analysis in *The Rhetoric of Reaction* (1991).

[81]This reference to interests and feelings obviously calls to mind *The Passions and the Interests* (1977) and Hirschman's related work. It also implicitly shows Eugenio's concern with the need to reconcile the interests and feelings of different countries within a federalist rationale — an idea that puts him close to Carlo Cattaneo; a theme that, characteristically, lay outside the vision of the Ventotene group.

tailored specifically to it." Here, then, is a way to untangle the knot.

We now come to the second reason why, at Ventotene, the question took on "a novel aspect." Colorni continues: "What also urged us to give autonomous prominence to the federalist proposal was the fact that existing political parties, tied to a history of struggles fought within the confines of each nation, are by habit and tradition accustomed to defining all problems on the tacit assumption of the existence of the nation-state and considering problems at the international level as issues of 'foreign policy' to be resolved through diplomacy and agreements between various governments."

This mode of operation, still current today, certainly cannot be changed from one day to the next, the reader will doubtless observe. But as Colorni warns, "this point of view is partly the cause and partly the consequence of the attitude mentioned above whereby, once power has been seized in one's own country, it is assumed that agreement and union with similar regimes in other countries will automatically come about without the need for a political struggle expressly dedicated to this end." So the one attitude can't be changed without changing the other — an indicator of the depth of the change, both international and domestic, that must be brought about in order to effectively confront the problem of nationalism and its tragic consequences. Because nationalism must indeed be placed in the dock.

"The authors of the present writings," Eugenio continues, "[. . .] held the deep-rooted conviction that anyone who wished to pose the problem of the international order as central to the current historical era and treat its solution as a necessary premise for solving all our society's institutional, economic and social problems, would have to extend this point of view to all issues concerning internal political contrasts and the attitude of each party, even regarding the tactics and strategy of the daily struggle."

12. This is a step that even today leaves the reader breathless. Once you have got hold of this key to sorting out the problem, thinks Colorni, you have to stick with your decision, giving it priority over every other aspect of political action — and it is here, in my view, that the most original aspect of the Ventotene formulation lies.

"All issues," Eugenio writes, seeking to meet the political problems of his time halfway, "from constitutional liberty to class struggle, from planning to gaining power and using it, take on a new light when articulated starting from the premise that the primary goal[82] is *a united international system*."[83]

What should we think, then, after all this time, of this conclusion that shifts the focus of political action into historically new and to a great extent uncharted territory?[84]

First of all, that this is an innovative political consequence that follows logically, almost inevitably, from the premise. In this regard, we see how the rebel philosopher (Eugenio) supports without reservation the position taken by the new brand of professional politician (Altiero) and the warrior-economist (Ernesto) on this decisive point. It could be said that he strengthens it *ipso facto* — with his theoretical authority.

Eugenio was also perfectly aware that to become a reality, this turning point had to permeate every aspect of politics — and herein resides the great political effort that was required. It is a daring thesis that at first glance may appear to be a simple Pindaric flight of fancy — especially when observed (as we do today) after such a long time. But it should be pointed out that for Eugenio (and later for Albert[85])

---

[82]There is a surprising concordance here with what Albert wrote from the other side of the world in California (Hirschman 1945) and later considered "infinitely naive" (up to a point — I in turn argued: Cf. Meldolesi 2013, Chap. 3, 2014, chap. 4 and "Long is the Journey . . ." n. 1, www.cornihirschman.org).

[83]"Even political maneuvering," Colorni continues, "— aligning oneself with one or another of the forces at play, highlighting one catchphrase or another — takes on a very different significance depending on whether the essential aim is to seize power and implement certain reforms within the ambit of each single state, or to create the economic, political and moral prerequisites for the establishment of a federal order that embraces the entire continent."

[84]There had been certain other proto-federalist European movements and experiences — such as those of Jean Monnet in World Wars I and II. But a federalist rationale deployed at a continental level from Italy (and from Germany) undoubtedly took on the features of a discovery, allowing, according to Eugenio's philosophy, a great step forward in the redefinition the European scenario (and consequently for all of humanity, as we shall see). If I am not mistaken the point is precisely this. Following the reasoning Albert (1981) would call "trespassing" (applying in one field the results obtained in another) Eugenio again proposes in politics part of what he learned studying the natural sciences.

[85]"Eugenio had too many ideas," Hirschman once told me at the end of the last century, meaning (presumably) too many to be able to develop them adequately. I long believed that, on the contrary, his enigmatic statement was intended simply to call attention to his own elaborations. Now, however, commenting step by step on Colorni's preface, I see the great number of ideas of Eugenio's that are actually at the origin of Albert's vast and

the energy required for such a change was in all probability hiding in the turning point itself.[86] It is the inversion, the reversal of the point of view that is important. So much so that this is where the energy has to be concentrated to open the doors to the future. Hence Colorni's support for the political process that had just then led to the birth of the European Federalist Movement — the forerunner of the initial European brotherhood that, however partial, imperfect, and born in the shadow of the Cold War, actually came into being in the postwar period.

On the other hand it is also true that this injection of federalist spirit did not by any means extinguish the issue, nor could it. This was not least because the Ventotene group's need to highlight the federalist dimension of political reasoning, until that moment unprecedented (and thus hidden), had the medium- and long-term effect of setting in motion *a new type of interaction* between the international and European, on one hand, and the domestic aspects of political action.

This in the sense that, while the perhaps unconscious neglect of the problem allowed nationalism in its various forms to prevail, this internal-external dialogue, once set in motion, has generated (and will continue to generate) a process of action and reaction that is part of our collective life. Which means that if it worked the way it ought to, this inversion of a trend, far from being a Pindaric flight of fancy, might just be a pole star.

13. We now come to Eugenio's third point. "Yet another reason — perhaps the most important [why the federalist idea is once again significant] — is the fact that while the ideal of a European federation, the precursor to a global federation, may still have seemed a distant utopia a few years ago, it now appears, at the end of this war, to be an achievable goal and almost within reach."

Every word here needs a brief comment. In the first place, in

---

remarkable scientific output. It is well known that Albert never wanted to write about Colorni's work, but he always recognized his great intellectual debt to Eugenio.

[86]The reference, of course, is to the famous argument on unbalanced growth that followed the publication of *The Strategy* (1958); and of the subsequent application of that point of view — from sailing against the wind (1984) to, finally, Chap. 19 of Hirschman 1995.

Colorni's vision, "the ideal of a European federation" would be "the precursor to a global federation" — because the Ventotene group still considered Europe to be the center of the world economic-political system. Only later — as I have mentioned — would it be realized that the war had transferred this "beating heart" to the United States, specifically to New York.

This altered the cards, because if Europe (mainly Germany; Berlin, in Colorni's mind) were no longer the center of the system, an eventual European federation would clearly no longer be the precursor, even hypothetically, of a global federation — the continental and global levels would be relatively independent of one another and would be discussed separately.

This being the case, the external-internal relation that Eugenio and his friends had identified in the form of federalism (vis-à-vis national states, with their attendant hierarchies, rivalries and tragedies) tends to be elevated and generalized as an all-encompassing interaction, between the world and the continents, among the continents themselves, between continents and regional federations, between these and countries, countries and their own regions, and regions and municipalities.

The key aspect, the antagonism between nationalisms and a federalist solution, must therefore be considered as part of this system of much more varied and complex relations.[87]

Let us look then at the second part of Colorni's proposition, according to which the ideal of a European federation, still a distant utopia some years before, presented itself at the end of the war as "an achievable goal and almost within reach." Now we know, of course, that it was nothing of the kind, that what they saw was a typical "fata morgana" mirage effect — one that emanates in the rising phase of some very important political-social processes (and which Colorni himself was aware of — cf. above, section 7). But we also know that

---

[87] Viewing the question from a theoretical point of view, the reading I am proposing has the advantage of avoiding what Eugenio and Albert would undoubtedly have rejected. That is to say, transforming (dangerously) a key aspect of reality (which the opposition between federalism and nationalism is) into a "single and unique" relationship — one that "rules the roost," so to speak. Unfortunately, it is precisely this error that many federalists throughout the postwar period have un-conciously fallen into.

such an illusion offers a precious glimpse of the future. That is, it discerns in those specific historical conditions a developmental trend that will light the way again and again.

Federalization (worldwide and therefore European as well) thus represented an alternative to nationalisms and their tragic consequences, something to be systematically pursued over entire historical periods as part of a process involving a much broader field of external-internal relations.

And not only that — with this decisive feature in mind (and thus viewed from this somewhat different visual angle), we can more readily appreciate the explanations of the phenomenon that follow in the text. "The complete reshuffling of populations," Eugenio writes, "that this conflict has provoked in all the countries under German occupation; the need to reconstruct on new foundations an economy that has been almost completely destroyed and to refocus attention on all the problems concerning political boundaries, customs barriers, ethnic minorities, etc.; the very character of this war, in which the national element has so often been overshadowed by the ideological element, in which small and medium-sized states have surrendered much of their sovereignty to stronger states; and in which the fascists themselves have replaced the concept of 'national independence' with that of 'living space': all these elements should be recognized as evidence that the federal ordering of Europe is more topical than ever before."

In a certain sense, Colorni and his friends were right to see in this list a trend toward the eradication of the nation-state and its concurrent replacement by a federal order. On the other hand, however, there was in their minds a sort of optical effect in which the current phase of immense military upheaval that they observed from Ventotene took the place of a historical era — the one in which we find ourselves today, still very far from the goal (and from the further developments that might follow it).

"Forces from all social classes," Eugenio concludes, "for reasons that are both economic and idealistic, may be interested in it. It can be approached by means of diplomatic negotiation and popular agitation, and by promoting the study of problems related to the issue among the educated classes, provoking *de facto* conditions of revolution from which it will be impossible to turn back; we can do this by influencing the upper echelons of the victorious states and spreading the word in defeated states that only in a free and united Europe will they be able to find salvation and avoid the disastrous consequences of defeat." In Eugenio's mind it was now all up to the European Federalist Movement, just established,[88] and to the political contingencies that would accompany the final phase of the war.[89]

14. "In the documents of the regime," Francesco Gui writes,[90] Colorni's political and intellectual image emerges strengthened in its precocious, steady, balanced and original, courageous and far-sighted conformation [. . .]. Even though convinced of the need for cooperation among all the forces ranged against the regime, and committed to militancy alongside the other forces in the fight for freedom, especially the communists, the professor remained entirely opposed to the arguments of those who saw the USSR as the country to guide the worldwide revolution or leaned toward a bureaucratic-repressive conception of power. This did not lead him, however, to retreat into factionalism, but rather to champion the potential of a socialist leadership on the condition that it should take the long view (the European federalist revolution) and of course have the ability to mobilize the masses. And that was not all, considering that Colorni did not hesitate to express his dissent, both rejecting Nenni's idea of a united front and undermining the basis of the communist 'myth' [. . .], not fearing that this would weaken the struggle or that he would suffer

---

[88]The passage continues: "The reason our Movement arose is precisely this. It is the pre-eminence, the precedence of this problem over all the others that afflict us in the period we are now passing through; it is the sure knowledge that if we let the situation re-solidify in the old nationalistic molds, the opportunity will be lost forever, and our continent will have no lasting peace and well being. All of this is what motivated us to create an autonomous organization whose purpose is to champion the idea of the European Federation as an achievable goal in the post-war period. We do not hide the difficulties of this [. . .]; but it is the first time, we believe, that this problem has been placed on the table of the political struggle not as a distant ideal, but as a pressing, tragic necessity." Obviously, what we referred to above as an "optical effect" is in play here as well, but this time in a positive sense. Because the "old nationalistic molds" have been in part modified to the point of generating (at least up to now) an era of peace in Europe — but not, unfortunately, to the point of making the "European dream" of Ventotene a reality.
[89]Further consequences of this reasoning are discussed below in the postscript.
[90]Gui 2010, p. 296.

the retaliation of his allied comrades."

At the same time, a careful reconstruction of the "courageous phase"[91] of Eugenio's life, his participation in the Roman Resistance, is outside the scope of the present task. Indeed, it does not seem to me appropriate to recall here the extraordinary experience of this versatile and tireless young socialist leader, capable of thinking, teaching, motivating, persuading and writing, as well as taking action. This is not because in speaking of Eugenio's topical politics one might ever consider passing over the bright page of Italian (European and world) history that he wrote in the circumstances.[92] But rather because, while still taking into account the complexity of these hair-raising events, the present work intends principally to show, for introductory purposes, how Eugenio's political writings, produced for specific reasons at particular moments in time, are nevertheless of interest today, and contain *general lessons* relevant to any time — ours included.

This, after all, seems to me to be the message that Albert

---

[91] As he himself defined it. In Rome Eugenio "moved about with the identity card of a Polish doctor"; "he felt alive, liberated from the perennial condition of inertia" his internment had condemned him to. According to Sirio Lentini, "he was enthusiastic about his own political struggle and the federalist idea" (Tedesco 2014, pp. 150 and 170–71).
[92] Re-evoked in often enlightening ways by comrades in arms like Leo Solari 1964, 1980, 2004; Claudio Pavone 2004, 2010; Giuliano Vassalli 2004, 2010 (cf., below, Ventura 2010 and Gerbi 1999, Chap. 7). "It may seem strange," writes, for example, Claudio Pavone (2010, p. 206), "that while distributing underground newspapers and preparing for an insurrection, a person could still speak of the great problems that had afflicted mankind over the centuries. And yet this was one of the exhilarating characteristics of the situation; the charm that Colorni held for two young people like Lopresti and myself came from our seeing in him the symbol of that fusion. His attitude towards us was affectionate and open, and we could speak to him about any problem that concerned us. He was barely ten years older, but in our eyes he held the fascination of an old anti-fascist militant who had known prison and internment and had intellectual prestige as well." "You cannot have a true perception of the character of his [Colorni's] political itinerary," writes Leo Solari (1980, p. 22), "[. . .] without trying to see how that itinerary also reflected the spirit in which he faced other activities as well, and more generally, life — a spirit that was constantly under moral tension, and thus pushed him into strict moral rigor towards himself; a spirit that was reflective, troubled, investigative, introspective, and which at the same time tended toward a coherent personal commitment to action; an anti-dogmatic spirit, anti-conformist in everything and also iconoclastic, but not out of a proud desire to be contradictory, but rather for love of the truth and an eagerness to get to the bottom of everything, in exploring new directions, in 'seeking what is new'; a spirit irreducibly devoted to the idea of freedom, driven not only by a conceptual construction, but above all by a natural vocation to respect the way others feel and think."

Hirschman wanted to give me when he taught me to think of Eugenio as if he were still present. Or when, on the occasion of the sixtieth anniversary of Eugenio's martyrdom, he wrote to Nicoletta Stame and myself a *petite* phrase: "I am grateful to you for renewing your friendship with Eugenio Colorni."[93]

To renew that friendship once again, I would like to show, by way of example, that alongside the many suggestions cited, there are many additional ideas in Eugenio's work that are extraordinarily fertile for tackling today's problems and properly guiding them toward resolution.

As a first experiment I would like to "rake over" several passages on fascist secondary schools,[94] first of all with reference to how Eugenio taught (and how teaching ought to be done).

"The antifascist professor," he writes in 1937, "can earn the respect and gratitude of his students if he explains to them in a way that is objective, historical and scientific what these things that they are expected to idolize really are and, even more importantly, what the things are that they are expected to revile. Left in total ignorance about these things — and this quite often happens during lessons in history or corporate law — the students have to ask the professor what liberalism or socialism or communism refers to. Explaining these things clearly and ubiquitously is not only possible, it is the official duty of the schools. And when students know and understand them, this is already a formidable element of propaganda against fascism."

And later: "The word 'homeland' has so often been dragged through the mud of fascist propaganda (and for that matter by all reactionary propaganda), it has been so cynically used for supposedly righteous purposes, and it has with such deliberate skill been used to sell ideologies of selfishness, social oppression, and international plunder, that all socialists and antifascists now hesitate to pronounce the term [. . .]. It nevertheless remains a word that carries the evocation of a certain ideal and finds an immediate heartfelt response, especially among the middle classes. It is a word that young people have since their childhood been in the habit of pronouncing with

---

[93] In Meldolesi 2004, p. 35.
[94] Colorni 2019, p. 38 and 39.

devotion, as a symbol of everything pure and unselfish. Are we to allow this word to be stolen by the people's enemies?"[95]

15. This is all very well, the reader might think at this point. But these are statements that preceded Eugenio's "conversion" to federalism. Does it make sense to repeat them *post factum*? Not only does it make sense, I would answer — it is essential to a true understanding of his point of view.

Indeed, he adds that ". . .the best way of giving a socialist or antifascist history course is to teach it in as complex and complete a way as possible, including all its social and economic connections; to see for example beneath the feudal economy and its derived social problems the substratum of the respective positions of the Empire and the Church and the culture that derived from them; to study the City-States, the *Signoria,* Humanism, the Renaissance, and the Reformation in relation to the new forces of the nascent bourgeoisie [. . .] It is only when it has become a matter of course that historical facts and political ideologies are seen to be tightly bound to the social and economic world from which they arise, that students can be trained in a serious and concrete vision of the current political reality[96] [. . .]. Only in this way can the origins of nationalism be sought in the ideologies of Bismark and of France in the early 20th century as distinct from the national unification movements of the 19th, showing the vitality and historical justification of the latter, and making it clear how today, now that national unification has arrived, the same words are being used and the same ideals exploited for purposes quite different from those that gave rise to them [. . .]. This is the only way young people will come to understand how it is that in a Europe in which national problems have been almost completely resolved, the only point in stirring up national feelings [. . .] is to distract attention from the real burning question of the age: the social problems within each country. This way they will also understand

---
[95]Cf., on the other hand (in n. 22 above and in the article "Problems of War": Colorni 2019), what he had already written in 1935 about national feelings.
[96]Colorni 2019, p. 42. Here in particular one can sense Eugenio's effort to make himself understood; and thus to make contact with the reader's political culture and at the same time to reformulate some aspects of it.

how, in the area of relations between one country and another, an ideology of all against all can be replaced with the ideology of cooperation of nation with nation, leaving to each the chance to resolve its own internal contradictions. This is the only way to set an ideal before the eyes of the young that includes the knowledge that they indeed belong to a national community, but that it has a function and meaning in the larger arena which is the human community."

So we see that Eugenio's adhesion to federalist ideals at Ventotene was the natural development of the point of view he held at Trieste. We see that his federalist struggle against European nationalisms (and imperialisms) was not only valid in itself — it also had the purpose of freeing progressive political energies within the different European countries; a prelude to the development of a new interactive (and iterative) external-internal back and forth process in each country, in Europe as a whole, and in the entire world — as a driving force for change. And this aspect can be captured, in my opinion, by linking together the two articles that Eugenio published before his death: "Administration or Revolution," and "Revolution from Above?"[97]

This may help us begin to grasp the moral of the question, which is to say that reflecting on Colorni's socio-political positions (and on his scientific, philosophical, methodological, etc. positions as well) has great value. First and foremost it means arming yourself, preparing a range of different arrows for your bow and being ready to deploy them as a source of inspiration, as a way of setting in motion (and persuading others to set in motion) the future of humanity.

16. Let me return for a moment to Eugenio and Altiero's 1943 debate over their divergent hypotheses concerning the postwar period, which seem so far from our experience. Indeed, the conjectures they advanced at the time did not come true — the expected German revolution (dear to Colorni) failed to materialize, while — for different reasons — neither Russia nor England played a pivotal role in the launch of Europe.[98]

---

[97]Colorni 2019. My reading of this relationship may be found in Meldolesi 2013, pp. 167 and ff.

[98]Even the debate between mass and individualist society today seems largely outdated. (This

What happened instead was the "revolution from above" that Eugenio had feared. The little Europe we have known up to now was set in motion by the six founding nations (Italy included), under the aegis of the United States during the Cold War.[99] Finally, it is also true that with the fall of the Wall (and of communism) things changed; and that the seriously disappointing European situation we have now lived with for so many years suggests that we should once again be asking ourselves what can be done.

Even on this point Colorni still speaks to us — for example, when he suggests that we create the micro-foundation of a firmly democratic society, that we consider the differing feelings of the European peoples (in addition to their material interests), that we concern ourselves directly with one another,[100] that we master the external-internal (and vice versa) relations of each country and the continent as a whole, that we rely on our own strength and on mobilizing the collective energy we ourselves possess (rather than on the strength and energy of others),[101] and so on.

"In the Europe of today," Eugenio wrote to Altiero in May of 1943, "Italy has a quirky, peripheral position, which can neverthe-

---

shows, if nothing else, the double aspect of these conjectures — on one hand they represent the need to light the way to the immediate future; but on the other their hypothetical, speculative, conjectural character implies that they will have to be continually verified and modified in the light of new information and an evolving situation. In addition, as I have mentioned, focusing on an analysis of the possible with regard to concrete conditions entails, at least in part, sacrificing the probable — that is, the attempt to predict the future to which so many have dedicated themselves throughout history, beginning with the Etruscans!)

[99] In continuing their struggle, Altiero, Ursula, and the other federalists undoubtedly played a significant role in fostering this pro-European evolution.

[100] A task which, as far as I can tell, has never been knowingly attempted, even at a pioneering (or experimental) level — unfortunately.

[101] Mass mobilization is in fact a recurring theme in these writings. Eugenio concludes his pamphlet on fascist secondary schools as follows: "In my view, the schools should not (as they often do) show or imply a limitless admiration for democracies like France or England or the United States. In spite of holding on to their democratic forms of government, these were nevertheless the countries that introduced the concepts of imperialism and colonialism to the modern world and in the recent Abyssinian crisis it was clear that attempts to defend them found no resonance in the expectations of even the most unprejudiced young people. Undoubtedly, siding with one or the other of these countries is appropriate in certain political situations. But the task we can perform in the schools is more general. And it would be neither fair nor possible, talking to young people who see things with innocent, unprejudiced eyes, to deny that the present balance in Europe, built as it was by capitalist countries, is intended to preserve these countries' commercial and colonial privileges."

less be decisive for unification. Anyone who wants to take action in Italy must accept this position, and cannot behave as if we were at the center." Which was true then, just as it is today. This implies, however, a serious commitment to our contribution to the common building project.

Here I see a twofold requirement: reconsidering Eugenio's contribution within the broader historical context of Italian federalism[102] and a consequent fine-tuning of the European objective, which cannot be restricted to what Colorni indicates in his Preface to the *Manifesto*[103] or those generally spoken of today (peace, being a global player, etc.). It has to concern, in my view, the Cattanean process of *civilizing* people — to be promoted in Europe, of course, but for "everyone."

"Our ideal," Gaetano Salvemini stated in concluding his speech to a famous federalist demonstration in Rome (27 October 1947), "was announced to the Italian people by Carlo Cattaneo in 1848. After the revolution in Milan, Vienna and Budapest had been put down by the troops of the Austrian home guard, Cattaneo, noting that Hungarians had wanted to be free, but at the same time wanted to dominate the Slavs and Romanians, and that the Viennese had wanted freedom, but also dominion over the Slavs, Hungarians and Italians, added, 'Only in the equality of fortune and in the necessities of war could those vain people understand that without brotherhood there is no freedom, that it is better to be free brothers than resentful servants. Every people must buy freedom with the sacrifice of barbaric ambition. Foreign people cannot be dominated without massive armies, nor without arrogant generals, who then use the strength of the conquered to oppress the winners. . . The seas are

---

[102]Cf. Meldolesi 2013, Chap. 1. In the 1930s, as Edmondo Paolini explained (1996, p. 206), "in Italy, federalist culture, mainly passed down from the Risorgimento, had been almost forgotten […], as it had in the rest of Europe as well, after the French defeat at Sedan at the hands of the German army, which had led, in the words of Benedetto Croce [in his *History of Europe in the 19th Century*] to the abandonment of all hope for a liberal European union.'"

[103]"These principles [basic to a free European configuration] may be summarized as follows: a single federal army, a single currency, abolition of customs barriers and emigration limits among the Federation's member states, direct representation of citizens in federal assemblies, and a unified foreign policy."

rough and swirling and the currents run in two directions: toward the autocrat or the United States of Europe.' This was the crossroads Cattaneo indicated," and where we still find ourselves today.

Postscript

As I see it, the interest in carefully re-reading and reconsidering the few pages of Eugenio's preface to the *Manifesto* lies not only — as I mentioned before — in comparing the generous aspirations of the Ventotene group with the present narrow-guage engine of the EU.

To me it seems even more important to see that the historical phase in which we now find ourselves at the world level, which has been given the name globalization, has been distinguished by a crisis of the Westphalian state.[104] Certainly this is true in a way that differs considerably from the situation surrounding the conflictual events of the last century — if only because the wars and guerrilla actions of our time have been (fortunately, up to now) of a regional nature. But this does not mean that it is useless to undertake a brief exercise in backward "mirroring"[105] concerning the period analyzed by the Ventotene group — to better understand the way things are and, if possible, to derive some useful guidance.

In the first place, even the present crisis of the nation-state should be viewed from a long-term historical perspective, which has its roots (I am told[106]) as far back as the 17th century, in the peace of Westphalia. In our own time, it has led to numerous adjustments (think of the consequences of decolonization, or the current multi-polar process which, until the arrival of President Trump, was gradually reducing the traditional hegemony of the US) and continues to show up as a historical propensity, taking on ever new guises.[107]

Even today, of course, federalism in its different forms (from loosest to strictest, from most local to broadest) represents a decisive response to nationalistic rivalries and their consequences, as shown by the powerful processes of connection and interconnection we are

---

[104]Cf. Appadurai 1996, d'Aquino 2014, Bassetti 2015.
[105]Concerning this approach, cf. Meldolesi 2012, Chap. 2; and 2015, pp. 120–29.
[106]I refer to the explanation by Piero Bassetti 2015 (cf., also, d'Aquino 2014 and Meldolesi 2015).
[107]Geertz 1999, Meldolesi 2016a and 2016b.

immersed in at the global level[108] (which also correspond to structural processes).

Certainly, democratic federalism, in its many developed forms and external and internal variants, is a solution vastly preferable to nationalist centralism — even to the current "revised and corrected" version. But based on experience, it would in my view be naive and reckless to consider this (as is) to be "the cure for our ills." On the contrary, the fact is that during the course of globalization market forces have eroded borders and mixed populations (religions, cultures, etc.), and continually called into question the "prescriptions" devised over time at the institutional level. Case by case, it is possible that tendentially federalist solutions respond better than others to these processes, but the course remains unsettled — by its nature it tends to repeat itself and present recurring challenges to the technical and political ingenuity of the numerous dramatis personae tending to the health of human societies.

On the other hand, it is clear that the emergence of the external federalism that the Ventotene group was talking about could have set in motion an internal democratic federalism (as outlined in some of the passages examined above).[109] This is not to say that (to complicate the picture even further) the very existence of vast fields of interaction at the different levels of the global institutional system also means that progress on one side should (or not) be accompanied by progress on the other (or even by regress).[110] The researcher is thus presented with a broad dimension of the reality to be investigated in which the nationalism-federalism opposition is generalized on numerous levels as a 'meeting vs confrontation' alternative — an

---

[108] Cf., for example, the map of changes in Watts 2005, p. 236.

[109] Both of these — by an inverse relationship — could have been linked (although they actually were not: cf. Meldolesi 2013, Chap. 1) to the federalist tradition of Carlo Cattaneo — not as a necessary relation, but simply as a possibility. In fact, in its Risorgimento version federalism was proposed for Italy and then extended to Europe, whereas the Ventotene reasoning was basically the opposite.

[110] To revisit the reference to the various forms of interaction involved in unbalanced growth discussed repeatedly by Albert (cf., above, n. 86), it now seems clear that the relation is inverse — in the sense in which Eugenio's 1944 preface brings to mind, as we have seen, some of the developments studied by Hirschman; but then, when we seek to take the reasoning further, we are spontaneously led at the outset to construct the discourse drawing on Hirschman's explorations and reflections.

opposition that comes up again and again.

Finally, even if we were hypothetically able, under a system of federalisms, to dominate the many explicitly nationalist trends (and the parts that make them up — think of social and territorial hierarchies, rivalries, confrontations, etc.) that continually and heavily condition our lives, we still will not have got *outside* the whole issue, because a Chinese federal state could always come into conflict with an Indian federal state or an American federal state, and so on.

And so it becomes essential to abandon the whole idea of a single solution, of an objective as such. It is undoubtedly still crucial to keep alive the pole star — the Colornian idea of federalization at the world and European level as an alternative to nationalist rivalries. But it is also necessary to think about the process by which humanity progressively *masters* its own destiny, and about collectives that work toward the growth of this sort of awareness.

And here we discover that our pole star begins to transform into a constellation. Because to reach the desired results, federalism has to be accompanied by other key aspects of the human condition — such as liberty, prosperity, democratization (as an effective alternative to the reasoning of hierarchy and domination), culture, social justice, equality (gender included), the environment, brotherhood, generosity.[111]

---

[111] We see, then, that in our era a United States of Europe appears obsolete and unattainable if proposed (as it often is) simply so that we will be an important player in conflicts with the other "world powers." Our continent has by now definitively lost its traditional role of domination. But it could hypothetically acquire another — the role of champion of the pole star, or even, as mentioned, of its corresponding constellation (the Great Bear) — that is, defender of the best that the world metamorphosis now underway has to offer. Anyone aware of this possibility cannot help but carry it mentally into every field of relations, not least in order to pursue the progressive struggle, wherever it may lead.

*Appendix: "Documents on Eugenio Colorni in the
Central State Archives"*[112]

*"Documents on Eugenio Colorni in the Central State Archives" edited by
Giulia Vassallo and considered here, comes from the April-June 2009 issue
of* Eurostudium 3w *(p. 10–158). Thanks to other sources (Gui 2010, Coppa
2012), I was aware of the importance of these documents, but not that they
were now available online, carefully ordered chronologically. So as soon as
I had the chance I undertook to read them (which was often boring and repetitive, but also, now that I think about it, shocking) and I did learn some
lessons from it.*

1. Having been suspected for some time of antifascist activity (the Milan police had initially denied him a passport), Eugenio Colorni was closely followed by two infiltrators from the fascist secret police beginning in February 1937. One of these (who for unknown reasons was later arrested) had entered into Eugenio's relationship with Giuseppe Faravelli on the (innocent) initiative of the latter; the other was stationed in Paris.[113] At the moment of his arrest (8 September 1938), the fascist police were therefore fully aware of his political activities. They could not present the evidence, however, without exposing their informers — so that in a note of 13 December 1938, the director of the Police Political Division, Guido Leto, wrote[114] that "For obvious reasons, none of the abundant material gathered against Colorni could be used, since it was all supplied by

---

[112] Thanks to Amedeo di Marco for his invaluable assistance in this research.

[113] More precisely, from a 39-page memorandum (see p. 64–82 of the April-June 2009 issue of *Eurostudium 3 w*) sent from Milan on 30 November 1939 by the Inspector General of PS to the Ministry of the Interior, PS General Directorate, Political Police Division, it can be deduced that the police operation began during the second half of 1936, when Faravelli went to the the Paris police agent (Alfredo Cimadori, according to Sandro Gerbi, 1999, p. 92), obviously ignorant of his role, "so that he would provide him with the name of a comrade, resident in Italy, willing to serve as an address in the Kingdom [. . .] The choice fell on one of our informers in Trieste, considered particularly suitable for the purpose, both because he had served, in his time, in the ranks of the Republican Party, and because of a certain 'reputation,' which he undoubtedly continued to enjoy among the Julian anti-fascist element. This is the well-known Ca." — who thus began his hateful job as an infiltrated double-agent.

[114] See p. 14 of the magazine.

our agent in Trieste and the other residing in Paris."[115]

From this it was clear that Eugenio's denial of everything that could be denied was perfectly correct as a defensive position,[116] as was the legal battle he then initiated in an appeal based on the fact that the police had little or nothing against him that could be proved. And finally, it was precisely this "fact" that saved him from the Special Tribunal "to which he had initially been denounced," according to a dispatch by Lieutenant Colonel Giuseppe Benvenuti, Commander of the Territorial Legion of the Royal Carabinieri Group of Trieste.[117] In other words, aware of his unfavorable position, Colorni reacted appropriately and immediately, thus avoiding a twenty-year prison sentence (or worse); at the same time he launched a counter-offensive that would have extraordinary consequences down the road.

2. This was the beginning of a sort of "role-play" began whose logic needs to be clarified. Eugenio tirelessly exploited the embarrassing position of the police (who were unable to prove what they knew) through constant appeals, petitions and requests for authorization based on the juridical formalism of fascism, which was considered by the authorities in charge to be an essential part of its alleged legitimacy (and might also serve the regime's need for social consensus and offer them a possible chance to make a good impression, especially abroad, by showing clemency). The police, for their part, while perfectly aware of what was going on, tried to smother his initiatives by dredging up every last detail of the story, as shown

---

[115]"In interrogations," we read on p. 34 of the memorandum (p. 81 of the magazine) [see n. 113], "every connection that could even remotely compromise the position of the Ca. and above all that of the agent in Paris [. . .] had to be concealed. And since there is no news or circumstance that had not been learned by us through one or the other of the two, it is clear how little remained that could be used against Colorni. Naturally, in the absence of specific charges, he could not be induced to confess."

[116]In all probability this had been prepared in advance, based on experience, as the most logical reaction to such an eventuality.

[117]Cf. p. 36 of the review. This information is confirmed (on p. 55) by the Ministry of Education which, on 29 September 1939, informed the General Directorate of Secondary Education that "Prof. Eugenio Colorni, professor of philosophy and pedagogy at the 'Carducci' Royal Institute at Trieste, arrested and referred to the Special Tribunal for the Defense of the State, was suspended from his position effective 1 October 1938, XVI, without pay, indefinitely" (but regarding the more lenient attitude of the Carabinieri toward Colorni, cf. Vassallo 2009 p. 42–43).

in the memorandum of 30 November 1939, which accompanied his definitive placement under police confinement by the Provincial Commission of Trieste.[118]

Francesco Gui (2010, p. 298) was thus able to write that the documents from the Central State Archive, "in which it is possible to follow the case of Colorni's segregation, open an intensely bright window on the daily life of the Ventotene guest [. . .]. Reports, correspondence, petitions, and telegrams offer a view of apprehensive Italian and German family members involved in complicated endeavors, of unhappy little daughters [. . .] injured swallowing a hairpin [. . .], of doctors urged to relieve the suffering of Ursula, yet again about to go into labor (all of which allowed her husband to obtain permission leave Ventotene temporarily for the mainland), of trusted domestics authorized to go along in support because they were not Jewish, of officials often willing to grant permits and of Carabinieri with lenient views, of great philosophers of fascism not indifferent to the drama of a man with a nervous system apparently under stress, of sisters ready to write to the Duce." It seems in a way to be the playing out of a pantomime at which (in hindsight) it is all too easy to smile. But as I will try to show, it is much less easy to understand its actual meaning going forward...

3. In fact, two key points need to be specified. The first is that throughout this non-stop battle Eugenio Colorni tried continually to bend the "role-play" in his own favor, thus discovering (as far as I know for the first time!) a relationship analogous to the political correction to the theory of economic dependency theorized by Albert Hirschman in 1978 (which he would later attach as a new introduction to the 1980 edition of *National Power and the Structure of Foreign Trade* – 1945; and which, as he told me personally, has behind it a well-known page from Hegel on the relationship between master and slave[119]). On one side was Colorni, pressing constantly

---

[118]Cf. above n. 113 and 114. Particularly surprising is the detailed and in-depth knowledge, as shown in the memorandum, of the political positions held by Eugenio Colorni within the Socialist Party.

[119]Hegel 1977, p. 111–19.

with a multiplicity of needs and proposing appropriate solutions; on the other side the various competent authorities were obliged to answer him. While they were of course aware, off the record, of past events, they had no clear idea what to do, even just to get out of the awkward situation and find some way to silence him.

The second point is that by acting in this way Eugenio was able to probe the terrain of his antagonists and identify their points of disharmony — sometimes even the brittleness of the terrain itself — and expose the fault lines in an apparently compact apparatus, so that he could take advantage of existing inconsistencies and/or possible misgivings on the part of its protagonists. This also allowed him to appeal to higher authorities when he thought it would help. In this regard, Ursula's "plea" to the Ministry of the Interior of 20 April 1939[120] made a significant mark. It was in reality directed at Epifanio Pennetta, a police commissioner and close collaborator of the Chief of State Police Carmine Senise and a person Colorni (in all probability) considered "sensitive." Surprisingly, it had a partially positive outcome[121] — Ursula moved to Ventotene with her daughter Silvia Clara (and a maid in tow).

---

[120] Cf. p. 42 of the review. It begins: "[in ink] 20/4/1939 — XVII. Expedite this immediately [in pencil] With Pennetta." That is to say: the day after the presentation of Ursula's request, which is dated 19/4, it was decided to immediately expedite the paperwork through the Police Commissioner Epifanio Pennetta. The text continues: "To the excellent Ministry of the Interior Directorate General for Public Security. ROME. I, the undersigned Colorni Ursula born Hirschmann, wife of Prof. Colorni Eugenio, son of Alberto, who is currently under political confinement at Ventotene (Littoria), would like to appeal to the benevolence and the high sense of humanity of this excellent ministry to take into consideration the following request" . . . and so on.

[121] Partial, because Ursula's request to be reunited with her husband was accepted, but at Ventotene — not on the mainland as she had requested (cf. Ursula's letter of 1 July 1939 to Arturo Bocchini). And yet this caused a sensation, such that many years later, in the interview *Passaggi di frontiera* [*Crossing Boundaries*] (1993, p. 27–28; English tr. 1998, p. 68) Albert Hirschman recalled that in spite of Eugenio's arrest, Ursula remained in Italy "and was not persecuted. This is an example of how fascism was less inhuman than Nazism. When Eugenio was banished to the island of Ventotene, Ursula asked to be allowed to follow him. In general this was not permitted, but the police argued that 'this poor foreign lady must be allowed to rejoin her husband,' so she was allowed to go." It is difficult to estimate, in any case, how much calculation went into the effect this concession would produce — even internationally, since it concerned a young German lady.

4. With regard to this, a further aspect of the question requires clarification. In the passage cited above, when Gui speaks of "great philosophers of fascism who are not indifferent to the drama of a man with an apparently exhausted nervous system," he is referring to the philosopher of fascism and Senator of the Realm Giovanni Gentile. Eugenio had met him during a vacation at Forte dei Marmi (where the Colorni family had a house that was open to relatives and friends). As I hinted at already, Gentile, who appreciated Eugenio's intellectual capacities, had published a series that included an edition of Leibniz's *Monadology* for the middle schools, edited by Colorni (1934). After the arrest and internment of the prominent Milanese philosopher, therefore, it cannot be excluded that Gentile raised the issue with the government of easing conditions for Colorni — for reasons of friendship, but probably also to put right what he considered to be overreach on the part of the police (a public security force which, as explained above, was not able to sufficiently back up its accusations).

It is certainly possible that this is what actually happened — especially in the last stages of the affair, according to the reconstruction of events by Sandro Gerbi (1999, p. 186) and Giulia Vassallo (2009, p. 62–63), given the request for mercy from Silvia Colorni, Eugenio's sister, to Mussolini, and Gentile's intervention with the chief of police. But in following this road we risk losing sight of what was in reality a formidable lesson in applied possibilism. This is because the key to the issue is not in my view an intervention from above in Eugenio's favor (the actual importance of which we do not know[122]), nor the inefficiency or, more generally, the low quality of the apparatus of repression (as one would expect following Hirschman's 1978 reasoning recalled above in section 3). On the contrary: the deciding factor, if I'm not mistaken, is the remarkable behavior of certain functionaries — servants of the state — who, under the exceptional conditions created by the war, and for reasons at once humanitarian and political, reacted in a particular moment in a way that was out of step with the behavior of the regime.

---

[122] Because, given that a certain opening had been created for an act of clemency on the part of the apparatus of oppression, it is possible that the request for mercy was solicited (informally) as a required condition for the approval of such a provision.

5. This is what happened in the case of Marcello Guida, vice director (then director) of political confinement at Ventotene, linked to Eugenio by "tacit sympathy," who later, as director of the Ministry of the Interior, secretly collaborated with the socialist partisans in Rome, serving after September 8th as a "link" between Pietro Nenni and Guido Leto, and became a point of reference for Colorni (so much so that Colorni, mortally wounded by the Koch band, appealed to his rescuer, Alfredo Ciancarini, to inform Guida immediately[123]). It also fits the case of Lorenzo Chierici who, named Chief of Police in April 1943 in the place of his friend Senise,[124] upheld the agreements with the King intended to provoke the resignation of Mussolini. On 25 July, he put himself at the disposal of Senise who returned to the Viminale with an escort of 500 policemen.[125] After September 8, Chierici was arrested by the Nazi police and handed over to the fascists of Salò, who killed him without trial. It is also true in the case of Francesco Peruzzi who, as PS Inspector General at Milan Police Headquarters, had expressed his opposition to Eugenio's transfer to the mainland;[126] but then, appointed as Rome's commissioner of police, he was involved in the preparations for Mussolini's removal and managed the transition of power.[127] And it certainly fit the case of Epifanio Pennetta, who in his day had had a leading role in the Matteotti murder investigation (and after the war was awarded a high honor by the Italian Republic).

At the time of Colorni's internment at Ventotene, these people were aware, with Senise, of the difficult personal conditions the Colorni family were having to endure. Thus Eugenio, with Commis-

---

[123] Cf. p. 86 of the review and pp. 220 and 225–27 of Sandro Gerbi 1999.

[124] Cf. p. 147 of the review. Carmine Senise had been "unseated" by Mussolini because he was considered too soft regarding worker strikes.

[125] But then, arrested by the Nazis after 8 September, Senise was interned at Dachau. In his memoirs (1945) he maintained that he had "tried, at a crucial moment in Italian history, to preserve the autonomous role of the police with respect to the regime."

[126] On 20 September 1941 (see pages 122–23 of the magazine), accompanied by the following motivation: "A possible transfer of the internee in question from Ventotene to a town on the mainland could put him in a position to reconnect with fellow Jews and old comrades at a time, like the present, when we see the revival of the socialist movement in some centers in Italy and especially in Switzerland and France, where Colorni, with his political intrigues, had gained a certain celebrity and a large following of friends and accomplices."

[127] Cf. p. 91 of the review.

sioner Pennetta as a point of reference, was able to mount a full-scale campaign for his own transfer to the mainland, led by Ursula, the lawyer Farina and himself, supported by a swarm of arguments concerning the health of the children, his wife, himself, etc. The impression one gets from scrolling through these documents is that indeed, in successive waves, Colorni made use of every opportunity, hammering at this same key until he won his transfer to Montemurro and then to Pietragalla.

With regard to his own case, Eugenio undoubtedly counted on the possibility of certain shifts in the power relations inside the police force as a result of his numerous initiatives.[128] He probably counted on a "transmission effect" by which the news (publicly available after Ursula's arrival at Ventotene) that the family's affairs were getting personal attention at the Ministry[129] would produce favorable reverberations "down through the branches" of the public administration. But more than anything, in my opinion, he counted on the fact that the war and the regime's growing difficulties would create numerous cracks (and enlarge the existing ones) in the consciences of these same officials. Maneuvering within the folds in the repressive structure, Eugenio showed an almost incredible ability to identify and consciously act upon these fissures.

6. The first lesson to be drawn therefore is that we must avoid trivializing simplifications — e.g., the state is composed of officials and employees (and not only politicians). As Amedeo di Marco points out,[130] the story told here shows that the bureaucratic apparatus of fascism, as distinct from the government and yet conditioned by its own constraints (attitudes in part inherited from our Republic), "was often endowed not only with intellectual honesty (in its rigorous and not specious application of the law), but also with humanity (in the ability to find lawful solutions to ease the heavy repressive burden), as well as acumen (in seeing that this was the

---

[128]To the extent that — as mentioned above (cf. n. 126) — the decision in his favor was made in spite of the opposition of Francesco Peruzzi.
[129]Cf. above, n. 121 and 122.
[130]Personal communication of 1 May 2019.

end of an era and that the next had to be prepared for)." In this way, right from the moment of his capture, using his own anti-fascism and gradually testing the attitude of his overseers, Eugenio implicitly placed before the best servants of the state the choice between being simply blind instruments of vile repressive practices, on one hand, and on the other gradually opening to dialogue — albeit cautious and indirect — in a situation that (if nothing else) deserved recognition and respect.

Undoubtedly, this illuminates Colorni's extraordinarily prescient actions. Remaining aloof from the other internees at Ventotene, he devoted himself to studies of scientific methodology apparently unrelated to current political matters, all the while incessantly pursuing the campaign for his transfer, sending one message after the other to those responsible on a daily basis — this itself a political step, albeit indirect. This was decisive, because the regime's decline certainly did not escape the notice of the best officials, nor did the opportunity to connect implicitly (secretly) with the Italy that was to come.

On the other hand, this did not prevent other officials from hardening their own repressive behavior, or still others from mixing their own "command" style of fascism with the southern baronial tradition, etc. In other words, in this action of Eugenio's there was already a whiff of inter-Italian civil war. His great practical service was not just having in a sense heralded this; it was also that he acted to provoke it, like the Mazzinian heroes of the Risorgimento — he said — whose daring actions upset the balance of power among the forces in the field. Colorni was probably aware of the role these officials could (and should) play in the inevitable transition process.

7. All this helps us understand Colorni's torment at Ventotene — his difficult psychological condition. On one hand his conduct had to be above reproach, reflecting the image of the professor of philosophy wholly absorbed in his studies, the image that he had presented officially to the police authorities; but at the same time he suffered from forced inactivity, from problems of concentration, alternating periods of calm with other, more frequent phases of depression; and also, as we know, he engaged clandestinely with Altiero, Ernesto and Ursula in philosophical "dialogues" and in the

discussions that would lead to the famous *Manifesto*.

But at the same time, as we have just seen, Eugenio vigorously pursued an original personal and political strategy that seems almost "Promethean," but should be understood in the context in which it was actually carried out. Perhaps initially dictated by the "power of desperation," it is lucid nonetheless. It carried a high degree of risk (which was progressively calculated), but above all of uncertainty — in the sense that the war, after repeated warnings, had actually broken out, creating untold scenarios and opportunities for the internees.

Eugenio held on. It was a miracle of "virtus et fortuna," to quote Machiavelli. Not least because Colorni did not find it easy to clarify and share his point of view — even with his wife. Ursula was in fact his accomplice, but given that she was a German citizen, it is likely that she didn't completely understand the logic of his actions and their institutional and political aims — so that she felt estranged from them, if not (I would surmise) actually exploited. In other words, Colorni's inspiration, choices and practical coherence came at a cost that in all probability he had not initially taken into account, but which he then had to accept, confirming, as we shall now see, his extraordinary determination.

8. And so we arrive, the reader and I, at the last — and much thinner — group of documents, those that cover the year and a half Eugenio spent confined at Melfi. He had to deal with a *Podestà*, Michele Pastore — a local party hierarch more interested in being in command than in applying the law. Witness the episode of displaying the flag that Ursula spoke of in the columns of the *Repubblica* (12 October 1986 see below). The Podestà had not received authorization to denounce Eugenio to the judicial authorities, and in any case the terms of his confinement "required that he not conduct any manifestation of a political nature" (which displaying the flag would surely have been). Hence his acquittal (with amnesty for the crime of contravening the order of the Podestà).

Colorni set up a home. He took care, working through Ursula and Commissioner Pennetta, not to be moved again, while at the same time cautiously resuming his clandestine activity by meeting with Franco Venturi and Manlio Rossi-Doria. But on 19 April 1943, when the prefect of Potenza transmitted to the center a report from the CC RR Lieutenancy Command of Melfi[131] to the effect that Eugenio had contracted numerous friendships, was giving private lessons to young anti-fascists, and was dodging surveillance in clandestine meetings with internees, the ministry took measures to move him again, this time to Pietragalla. From this point events moved rapidly. With ministerial authorization, the prefect of Potenza "appealed to the Podestà of Melfi to have the internee accompanied to the administrative center for radiological tests. The Podestà, instead of doing so, provided the aforementioned internee with a compulsory expulsion order. He did not appear at the Potenza Police Headquarters, making himself untraceable,"[132] so that he could go to Rome.

Finally, on August 10th (and therefore after July 25th) Colorni asked to speak with Commissioner Pennetta. On the 16th he was released from obligatory confinement, and on 31 August the Rome police commissioner ordered "appropriate surveillance" of him (care of Pontecorvo, via Livorno 25).

(May 2019)

---

[131]Cf. p. 149 of the review.
[132]Rather than puzzling over why this happened, it seems to me simplest to hypothesize that, in view of the way things were going, the Podestà issued (illegally) the compulsory expulsion order to prevent Colorni from returning to Melfi; and that Eugenio was quick to take advantage of it.

Part I

1. Letter of Agostini to the Directorate of the Italian Socialist Party[1]

Anti-fascist Alliances, Tactics, and Political Parties

February-March 1936

Dear comrades,

I have recently had occasion to read some excerpts from the socialist and communist press on the discussions that have for some time been going on between our two parties concerning organic unity and relations with the liberal and democratic parties.

I want to offer some of my observations on the subject, no more than my personal opinions, which I previously expressed to the comrades at the Italian Center, and which only distance prevents me from discussing with them again now, before sending them to you. In any case, from the discussions we have had, I have reason to believe that these opinions are not isolated but are shared by other comrades. I am sending them to you as an expression of my own personal position and at the same time to the Center as well, as a voice in the discussions that ought to lead the Center itself to adopt definite positions.

The points under discussion are essentially two: 1) the position concerning the bourgeois parties and the scope to be given to alliances with them; 2) the work to be done by the proletarian parties (a mass action or training of cadres).

On the first point, I think that the variety of agreements and alliances being undertaken among the various parties (united action, organic unity, popular front government, union of anti-fascist forces, etc.) has led to a certain confusion of ideas. We can identify four types of unions between parties — and these should be kept clearly distinct.

1. *Alliance with any anti-fascist party or group, of whatever tendency or type.* This has to be based on extremely generic catchwords (the slogans from Brussels) and limit its scope of action to bringing

---
[1] Letter published in AA.VV. (1963), *Documenti inediti dell'archivio Angelo Tasca*, 188–92.

about the fall of fascism and the conquest of basic democratic liberties, the necessary basis for any party's activity. (We cannot speak in this case of an alliance with fascist opposition elements, since no one who agrees to a plan to destroy fascism can be called fascist, even a party member). On the other hand, an alliance of this type cannot be allowed to go even one step beyond the conquest of democratic liberties. Any agreement on a program, any preparation — even provisional — of government projects must be rejected by all proletarian parties in the most absolute terms. Any departure from this principle would be to fall into old errors that would inevitably lead to reformism. (Another thing entirely is a popular front with the middle classes, of which I will speak below.) The operations of this single anti-fascist front will have to take place (as they do already) through the formation of mixed committees whose actions can only be political (and therefore illegal) and who will be the ones to launch the signals for an immediate end to the war and the destruction of fascism. Many factions of the bourgeoisie adhere to these principles. We have to remove any illusions they may have, however, concerning a possible joint transfer of power and we must avoid any negotiation based on reciprocal program concessions. Our path will immediately and inexorably deviate from theirs as soon as the elementary objectives we now share have been achieved.

2. *Popular front with the middle classes.* This is what we see now going on in France and elsewhere. It is conditioned by a particular political situation and can only be achieved in certain specific cases. It is a union of the proletarian parties with certain factions of the petty bourgeoisie and the middle classes and their parties, with a unified program and the expectation of taking power together. This sort of front is not at all relevant to the current situation in Italy. It is achievable only in particular conditions that concern the political crisis in a democratic regime — one of which, for example is the prospect of a revolutionary situation that develops in a direction that is not at first socialist. Conditions of this type absolutely do not exist today, nor is it at all foreseeable that they will. It may be that the situation that develops with the fall of fascism will lead us into a popular front; perhaps we will instead be able to avoid passing through such an in-

termediate stage. In any case, we are not in a position today to predict the eventual nature of our policies with respect to the middle classes or what forms our alliance with them will take.

It does not seem to me that the comrades of the Socialist Center have maintained the distinction between these two types of agreement, which have nothing to do with each other. Suggestions from the French popular front have perhaps led them to assume "popular front" attitudes in a very different situation not at all open to such a solution. An agreement with the liberal anti-fascists, who expect fascism to fall exclusively as a result of developments in the international situation, whose anti-fascism has always been negative and who are thus temperamentally inclined toward mergers, is undoubtedly the easiest to achieve here in Italy; and given the passive base they depend on, it is clear that discussions with them will often slip into speculation about what will happen "after." In these conversations we must not, however, allow ourselves to be dragged beyond the limits imposed by our own integrity. The Parisian editorial office's article in the *Nuovo Avanti!* of 1 February 1936 entitled "The Socialist Politics of Alliances and the Popular Fighting Front" is in fact based entirely on this.

3. *United action of the Socialist and Communist parties.* Here we enter into the second of the problems on the table, the work to be done by the united proletarian parties. Here again the differences derive from confusion about the different forms these unions can take. It is obvious that unity of action absolutely cannot be limited simply to an agreement pending the spontaneous fall of fascism. This would mean giving up in advance all influence on events and letting the revolution come down from above like some free gift. We cannot predict whether fascism will fall due to the force of external events or from an impulse that comes from within, from the working masses. Probably these two elements will meet in a relationship of mutual dependence. In any case, the one we can most effectively influence is the internal factor — that is, preparation for revolution. This is the essential task we must dedicate ourselves to, lest we should later find ourselves (even if the situation comes to a head following international developments) unprepared and cut off from the trust of the masses. And the slogans and catchphrases for this job must include

anything, anything at all that might arouse discontent and a sense of hostility toward fascism and the exploiting classes.

The nature of this sort of action is quite different from the generic anti-fascist activity referred to in n. 1 above. Its character is clearly class-based. It must involve all those who have suffered at the hands of fascism, capitalism and war not only as thinking beings, but personally, in their concrete interests and daily lives. The operation therefore ought also to appeal to those who are not a priori opposed to fascism; because the struggle against fascism is the consequence, not the premise of this action — the struggle is the final result of late-acquired awareness on the part of the masses that fascism means their ruin. Such action must make use of every possible means, legal and illegal, from partial economic claims to strike actions to mass uprising. While at other times small economic claims might possibly depress the people's revolutionary spirit and distract them from their final goal, the present Italian situation is such that the circumstances themselves render even the most minimal partial claim both political and revolutionary, inevitably connected in everyone's mind with the general situation, the war, and the coming end of fascism. The dangers of so-called "minimalism" or "economism" are now much less serious than in other situations. This action is the most important that we can accomplish, one that will concretely lay the foundation for the participation of the Italian people in their own revolution.

Concretely, in the present moment, what is the state of socialist and communist cooperation in this operation? The famous divergence over "mass action" vs the "formation of cadres" will be resolved as not so much an ideological question as an organizational problem of a technical nature. The communists often speak of a "combined front from the bottom" formed by the masses, in which socialist workers join in factory actions directed and led by the communists. Assuming that this actually happens, it is not at all what might be considered a united front. Any anti-fascist worker will always be likely to join and support action undertaken by other anti-fascist workers whether or not they belong to the same party; and this spontaneous collaboration, which has always occurred and always will in the present state of the political struggle, has nothing to do with an agreement concerning a stable and durable line of common political action, with jointly trained leadership — this is the meaning and essence of the United Front. The United Front has to express itself essentially in mass action, I agree, but it cannot be limited to seeking the endorsement of this or that group of workers from the allied party for a particular operation. It has to have a line, a stable foundation, a consistent operational direction — it needs "organs." Now it seems to me that the communists' insistence on mass action masks a certain lack of effort in the formation of these United Front operational organs and a certain inclination to make use of this expression simply to create at the base de facto unions in which they have a better chance of coming out on top. (In this I feel I must fault the communists for a spirit less than fully up to date with the turnabout that marked the 7th World Congress of the Comintern). And on the other side, the intellectual origins of the Socialist Center and its limited contact with the masses have caused mass action to be downgraded and have led to a push for the training of cadres. Mass action is, I repeat, the basis and foundation of our operations — but a true and productive collaboration between the two parties will not come about without the preliminary formation of organs that will guarantee it a coherent and regular path of development. Otherwise, we risk being outflanked by the masses, who even today all too often act spontaneously in ways that are disorganized and unproductive, and outside the influence of either party. (I will spare you the relevant quotes from Lenin's *What Is to Be Done?*). The difficulties mentioned above are chiefly due to the differing conformations of the two parties, which is a source of mutual distrust. Communism, based in Italy exclusively on mass action, with its executive committee in Paris and functionaries at its base who are strictly bound by party discipline and lack any real autonomy of action, will hardly agree to put its worker functionaries in contact with independent and autonomous intellectuals of the Socialist Center. (This is the only way I have of explaining the impossibility we have encountered in establishing relations with Communist leadership elements who are actually in contact with the masses, and are not simply functionaries specifically assigned to "work with the intellectuals" or have no relations with the rest of the party.) Now it seems to me that this reluctance ought to disappear once our party clearly shows, as I said earlier, that it does not mean an alliance with the bourgeois parties to be anything more than a simple "shared stretch of road" that ends as soon as the battle's immediate goals have been reached, and that no sort of governing agreement is contemplated; and the party must also show a firm desire to act with respect to the masses — to take an active part, that is, and not simply wait for developments that lead to the fall of fascism. These two points are not "concessions" to the Communist Party — on the contrary, they represent, in my view the line of conduct most coherent with the principles behind our action. But they are also a basis that removes any reason for disagreement between ourselves and the communists. Based on these principles we can expect more real and concrete cooperation from them, more comprehensive and stable contact that will allow a principled rather than intermittent agreement — one that will allow the close and profound exchange of ideas that will lead to organic unity between the two parties.

4. *Organic unity.* What must not be forgotten (and the communists forget this too easily) is that organic unity is the final and *urgent* goal of our efforts. The communists, it seems to me, are waiting passively for this simply to emerge as a product of the experience of our unified action. On the contrary, it needs to be hurried along in discussions and negotiations that proceed actively and include open debate. There is no element on which the distance between our points of view is so great that a common basis cannot be reached through sincere discussion. Mass action and fraternal collaboration in the daily struggle must serve as a foundation for these exchanges of ideas, but not as a substitute for them. On the contrary, wide-ranging discussions along with the resolution of some ideological differences can make our ties in practical operations stronger. For our part, discussions of this sort are of the utmost importance for the great practical results they can lead to, and we welcome them. We have already started laying the foundations on our own. And we look forward confidently and impatiently to the help and cooperation of our communist comrades.

Agostini

2. The Struggle within Fascism[2]

The new turn of events signaled by the latest manifesto of the Communist Party has sparked a variety of comments and debates among us. It might be useful for us to take a position, not only to clarify where we stand in relation to communist theory and tactics, but to establish certain points and guidelines for our work. The manifesto obviously represents an accentuation of the united front policy and collaboration with the middle classes set in motion at the seventh Congress. It is pointless to examine here whether and to what extent the slogans issued by the CP in Italy are a translation of the same words issued in France. What matters to us now is their value and their applicability in the Italian situation, regardless of how and by what procedure they were devised.

At the center of these new directives lies the policy of addressing the fascist masses directly using catchphrases that do not disturb their way of thinking and that identify their enemy not as fascism per se, but rather as the upper classes, which they do not directly identify with fascism — catchphrases that are more accessible to the masses and the petty bourgeoisie, that are less dangerous, that allow for a reawakening and almost a rediscovery of the class struggle within fascism itself, and which promote this struggle initially as something that doesn't immediately contradict fascism. Only later, in a more evolved state, will it be recognized that the destruction of the upper classes or of the upper bourgeoisie is only possible through the destruction of fascism.

On this general point of view we are in full agreement. It implies the recognition that in its social makeup, in its organization, in its mindset and ideology, fascism can no longer be identified with the upper bourgeoisie; that it is a force supporting big capitalism, but it is not big capitalism. And it also implies that just as the fascists used language against us that was meant to confuse us and to derail

---

[2] This article was published — with no pseudonym — in the 31 October 1936 Paris edition of *Nuovo Avanti!*

the struggle from the issue of class onto more generic and muddled terrain where they could beat us because we were unprepared, in the same way we have to make use of this vague and uncertain terrain to reintroduce the notion of class as something new, using the pretext that it doesn't conflict with any of the official and proclaimed ideals of fascism.

Mass Struggle

These are concepts that we have long advocated, and it is in fact the communists' support of them that has made it possible for us to work together. But we would do well to remember (and this is perhaps not sufficiently clear in what our communist comrades have written) that adopting fascist language and generically addressing the Italian people does not mean giving up our class-based position, even as a tactical artifice. We do not want even to appear to preach any doctrine of conciliation between the classes. But we do want to define the current form of the class struggle in Italy under fascism as the struggle of the overwhelming majority of the population against a tiny minority of big capitalists. We must always keep in mind that approaching the middle classes does not have to mean anything other than attracting them to a class position alongside the proletariat, using whatever words are most appropriate in the concrete situation. The misunderstanding seems also to be perpetuated by the communists' reluctance to speak of big capitalism as a class, limiting themselves instead to mentioning by name some of its main representatives. This attitude may be dictated by conspiratorial caution and by a concern to pass such language along to the masses in a less dangerous way, but it makes it increasingly necessary to clarify to the masses themselves that these names are no more than examples, and that these magnates of industry, landed property and finance are only a few exponents of what is a strong and organized class, with its own organs, instruments, policies and alliances.

Once this broad adhesion and these reservations have been clearly established, what remains is the problem of application. In a concrete sense, how shall we go about spreading this message? What should our approach be in offering it to the working masses and the middle class? In what capacity should we present ourselves to them?

It seems to me that three possible positions can be distinguished.

An Unattainable Position
1. The position taken by the communist manifesto is to turn to the fascists with the offer of an alliance. Take advantage of their disappointment, show how fascism has betrayed their aspirations and incite them to fight alongside us to achieve the goals set by fascism itself back in its early days. This position to me seems absolutely unattainable in our relations with the masses. Approaching the fascist workers and petty bourgeois fascists and inviting them to cooperate with socialists or communists as such, or talking to them about a socialist or communist struggle in which they ought to take part may be conceivable in a democratic country, but in a regime of fascist dictatorship it is absurd. I can't imagine that our communist comrades could even for an instant have deluded themselves that a large-scale action might be possible in which a communist, identified as such, could reach out to a fascist (even one who was disappointed and discontented) and offer the party's collaboration in a joint action. Such a move would take him directly to prison. This is why the language in the manifesto needs to be interpreted as a generic statement of a generic political line, unusable in any direct contact or in the press reports accompanying a concrete action.

The 1919 Program
2. Identify as fascists, advocating the struggle against the upper bourgeoisie in party circles, emphasizing that the program of 1919 carried anti-capitalist language, and supporting any movement within fascism that tends toward the implementation of such language. This is the position of the so-called "corporatists" — adherents of movements which, in greater or lesser degrees of good faith, attempt to guide fascism toward social revolution from within, under its own power. That we need to stay close to these movements, to study them, support them and mingle with them to prevent them from being (as they have been until now) simple pawns in Mussolini's game — this much is evident. Up to now such movements have had the character of small cliques of ambitious intellectuals, with various gradations; from the self-styled unorganized communist

who claims to want to conduct the fight within the fascist party (and in practice ends up with a career and forgotten ideals) to the enthusiastic, intelligent and sincerely deluded fascist who believes he can lead the party onto the path he has discovered to be the right one. For us it is clear that this second type is the most interesting. But such movements in any case have little to show for their efforts — leaves of absence, initially even subsidized by Mussolini, who used to love to paint himself as a socialist, were brutally suppressed at the beginning of the Abyssinian enterprise and have yet to be resurrected. None of the leaders behaved decently in the face of this repudiation — they all bowed their heads and asked forgiveness and, when faced with the alternative of internment or enlistment in Abyssinia, they chose the second and then tried to go into hiding. In any case they will probably be back; our task will be to extend these movements into more lively environments in the economic domain, to cause them to penetrate trade union spheres, and to ensure that they come into contact with the working classes. In these environments, the significance of adherence to the program of '19 may not take the form of an agreement between ourselves and them, but rather of a reaffirmation of that program by fascists who believe in it and demand its implementation by their party. It is true that it has never been taken seriously by anyone, but this does not prevent its being revived. And if this is prohibited (which is more than probable), it will be an opportunity to expose once and for all the true reactionary character of fascism, and to demonstrate that it is constitutionally incapable of carrying out the most elementary social reforms.

Illusory Possibility

But we have to try and make people realize as quickly as possible that these hopes for the eventual evolution of fascism are illusory, and that the repression I spoke of might have produced a very different outcome if the affected groups had not been small deluxe cliques but rather had been an integral part of the social fabric of the nation. In that case such they might have contained the steadfast, honest and determined people who could have profited from the lesson and drawn from defeat the necessary revolutionary consequences.

3. The third position, the only one that can really be adopted on a large scale among the working masses with a chance of success, calls for propaganda not among the fascists, but in the context of fascism. Italian workers, although almost entirely non-party members, nevertheless come under the influence of fascism in after-work recreation, trade unions, schools and sports clubs. This influence does not make them militant, but it does make them people for whom fascism is an established condition to be passively put up with, something they do not always see as a direct oppressor. The links between fascism and capitalism are hidden, twisted and confused by official propaganda in such a way that it is often difficult, for young people especially, to see clearly that the regime is the main support of the ruling class. Our operations will have to try and raise awareness of this by accepting the political state of affairs and directing workers' attention towards goals that are more obvious. We must not approach them with the sort of aims that they see as fascist, socialist or communist, but rather as normal people for whom fascism is, as it is for everyone, simply the world we live in — a condition that we cannot help but accept, and to which direct opposition would be madness. We need to ensure that the masses of young people are educated to see the class struggle as something independent, not involving an immediate collision with the regime. Fascism has never raised its flag in defense of capitalism, nor has it ever bestowed a halo of national sanctity on the magnates of finance. On the contrary, it proclaims its concern for the working class and poses as their defender. We must take advantage of this hypocrisy and lead a propaganda campaign against institutions or people (better institutions than people) it is not yet sacrilegious to offend. Let us promote action in support of claims that fascism has never officially attempted to deny. We will thus set the working masses on a path toward rediscovering the language of class with virgin eyes, as if it had never existed, without immediately incurring accusations of anti-fascism.

A Political Struggle
And this will not be a purely reformist movement aimed exclusively at achieving wage increases. The struggle against the ruling

class will be of a typically and essentially political character. This is the only way it can achieve its purposes of renewal and education. What is new about this compared to previous positions is that the recognized enemy will no longer be fascism as such, but rather its master, the capitalist.

For this it is not in any case necessary or useful to conform to fascism. It is enough to live in its territory and recognize it as the normal state of existence, advocating change within it but not losing sight of our own existence and ultimate goals. We can thus create a post-fascist movement that does not present itself in the same way as the many parties fascism has eradicated, but rather as a development of the internal dialectic that will lead fascism inevitably to its end.

3. Letter of Anselmi to Joseph[3]

Political Function and Organizational Function

6 August 1937

Dear Joseph,

Following my letter of two days ago, I would like to present a number of concrete proposals which I believe represent the thinking of other comrades at the Center, and which Tasca substantially agrees with.

1) The recent arrests have shown that there was a defect in the composition of the Italian Center. In my view the error was that political and organizational functions were not differentiated and were entrusted to the same people. The Italian Center had control of virtually *all* the work in Italy, in all the cities. The comrades in charge knew all the soldiers on the ground and had contact with all the Party's business. This fact, a reflection of their splendid work and total dedication to the cause, is nevertheless what got them into trouble and allowed the police to carry out their huge raid and seize the most active and important centers. It also led to some confusion in the distinction between political and organizational work — for example, an extremely risky underground publishing apparatus of an ideological character (*Echi*) was set up locally when this could have been done abroad. In my view the function of the local press should be to produce immediate propaganda for the masses, the sort that requires extremely rapid circulation (this last is my own personal opinion; I didn't get a chance to discuss it with our friends at the Center). *Conclusion: The Center must remain active and be rebuilt as soon as possible.* It is an inescapable necessity for the practical results of our work; it is the body that underpins our decisive superiority over the communist organizations. But *the Center, as such, has to have a political, not an organizational function*. It has to be a body that is compact and agile, composed of people who have long been

---

[3]Letter published in AA.VV. (1963), *Documenti inediti dell'archivio Angelo Tasca*, 220–23. The earlier letter Colorni-Anselmi refers to has not survived.

in touch with the political situation and have maintained continuous contacts abroad. If possible these people should come from different Italian cities (but be able to meet periodically). Their business should be to draft policy directives for immediate transmission abroad. This way, the Center will not have to deal with organizational work (which does not rule out a member pursuing a personal organizational activity in his specific field). But organizational work, in short, should not be centralized in the Center. For organizational purposes, each group, each city, should have its own direct foreign contacts (for the reorganization of the work abroad see section 2). Each group should receive the Center's directives, printed material, etc. from abroad. In this way, the pressure on the Center can be relieved. All that's required is that one person in each group have a passport. And the Foreign Center, I repeat, will have to be modified. The leading elements in each Italian group *must not have any contact with any other Italian group*. Such contacts can be established among the masses, spontaneously, but a*mong the people responsible, in organizational work, watertight compartments must be established*.

In short, the work in Italy should be organized as follows:

Several different groups, in all the centers. In each group, one, two or three people at most responsible for the illegal work, which they will carry out in contact with the nearest Foreign Center. They will also be the editors of the local press, which will follow the directives transmitted from abroad and will have the character of propaganda rather than ideology. They can all participate in the work of ideological clarification either by communicating their views to some Center representative they possibly know, or by sending them abroad as personal opinions. Each of the directors of the base groups will maintain extremely cautious contact with elements from the masses, where possible bringing into play the spontaneity I spoke about in my recent article,[4] and will try to identify and set up, for each contact environment, *entry routes* for the press and for our catchphrases, which will then circulate by themselves. These catchphrases and local printed material will possibly have to be produced in collaboration with the communists, to whom these proposals about modes of mass

---

[4] Colorni 2019, ch. 2

distribution and the use of spontaneity should also be submitted. At the same time, even with the communists our group leaders should limit contact to a very few responsible elements.

Beyond the groups there should be an Italian Center — a body composed of a limited number of people who represent the various environments in which we have a political organization. The Center should meet with some regularity, maintain foreign contacts, be up to date with Party discussions abroad, and receive communist press reports. All Center representatives will maintain generic ideological, non-organizational, contact with core elements of their home environment or city. In view of the great scarcity of personnel, members of the Center can be allowed to carry out certain organizational activities in their local environment. *Under no circumstances, however, are they to make organizational contact with elements in other environments or cities.* They will instead attempt to legally penetrate the greatest possible number of environments and strata of the population, the point being to get an idea of the people's needs and states of mind. Then on this basis the Center will draft the directives for our political work in Italy; directives that will be transmitted abroad and will become obligatory for every Italian group. Each group will then receive these directives through its foreign contacts.

2) Work abroad. The latest arrests have shown that the error was not only internal congestion, but congestion abroad as well. Even abroad (that is, at the Lugano center), too many functions were concentrated in one place, and political work was confused too often with administrative work. In addition, the fact that all the work was centered at Lugano obliged us to concentrate all the internal work in Milan, with all the drawbacks I mentioned. And last but not least, the Lugano center is very well known to the police, who through it can follow all our moves.

Conclusion. All the political work will have to be concentrated in Paris. The border stations must be purely organizational. In the second place, we will have to give up on the single center for Italy, at Lugano or anywhere else, and replace it with a number of border posts that would be linked to groups reporting there. For these border posts it will not be at all necessary that comrades in Paris be mobilized to handle this exclusively. It will be sufficient to find dependable militants locally, Italian or even foreign, who would give reliable guarantees of their dedication, and who would commit themselves, possibly with some small compensation, to maintaining a press depository, handling the introduction of printed material into the country through local channels, corresponding clandestinely with Italian groups, etc. Divided up by regions, this work would require a limited time commitment from each of them, and they could do it as an activity marginal to their normal occupation. Briefly, organization abroad should happen as follows:

An office for Italy in Paris, under the Party Directorate, in direct contact with the Internal Center for discussing political questions, and in contact as well with the various border posts, which it will use for distributing printed material and directives, and which it will inspect periodically. This office for Italy, however, should not maintain any organizational contact with Italian groups. A certain number of posts in various border towns will maintain contacts, as I said above, with internal groups in cities near the frontier and other cities inside Italy. The people in charge of these posts should each have a precise responsibility, and it would therefore be appropriate that they be paid.

Posts of this type should be set up as soon as possible at the borders with France (Modane), Switzerland (*not Lugano*), Austria (Brenner for Verona-Venice), Yugoslavia (Sussak or Postumia). Any internal city could manage whichever frontier is most convenient in the circumstances (for example, Bologna for the Brenner, etc.). In addition, posts of this type could be established at ports where Italian ships stop before putting in at an Italian port (Marseilles, Tunis, Athens, Ajaccio, etc.). Coastal cities might also be used in this way (Naples, Genoa, etc.). This system will seem cumbersome to you, but in the end it is much simpler than the other one. Consider that up to now, to receive printed material we have had to resort to Milan, spending 150 lire for the journey, often not getting the material, and running grave risks; whereas there is someone crossing the frontier all the time. The only problem with my plan would be setting up the border posts. But I don't think it would be difficult to find a serious and trustworthy comrade in each city with a little free time for this. This person would receive a modest fee and there would be no danger involved. And if an Italian can't be found, we'll surely find a Frenchman, a Swiss, a Yugoslav or an Austrian. Get back to me right away so that something concrete can be set up before I leave. I'll be here for about another week.

Affectionately, your
Anselmi

For now I will keep the pseudonym Anselmi. But I will sign the articles I send with a new name each time. The last one was initialed D 4. The articles on the schools should be made into a brochure and sent abroad to various professors toward the beginning of the next academic year (November). But in any case, remove the signature Agostini in the brochure. In Milan I gave a list of professors the brochure could be sent to. I don't know if it got to you. Anyway, if you send the brochure, don't send it to the city where I live, and maybe not to Milan either.

4. Letter of Anselmi to Joseph[5]

Anti-fascist Political and Organizational Activities

9 August 1937

Dear Joseph,

I'm answering you straightaway. I want nothing more to do with the disputes about us accusing you of being reckless and you accusing us of being timid. In my view the decisions the Directorate has already worked out with you, which are soon to be implemented, are fully satisfactory in terms of your needs and ours. In the meantime I think you received my previous one[6] and and that you are favorable to the border post project.

When you're in Paris a month from now I hope you'll take care of this reorganization of the work abroad. I think it will give us much better security guarantees.

This is in my view the concrete application of the ideas expressed in the article on spontaneity and the speech to the Congress (Tasca would like to see it, and I ask you to send it to him).[7] The greatest difficulty for the new organization is the financing, but Tasca reckons even this problem will be solved. I'm sending you some general directives, which I worked out in a hurry and are therefore perhaps incomplete, but they will give you an idea of how I understand the job.[8]

In my opinion (and Tasca agrees) the Erba group absolutely cannot constitute the new Center. This is an extremely corrupt and subnormal group. They can work, as long as they keep to themselves and do not establish contact with other groups. So we would ask you to maintain the contacts you have in this group, but not to give them any contacts here with us. We will set up direct contact with

---

[5]Letter published in AA.VV. (1963), *Documenti inediti dell'archivio Angelo Tasca*, 243–44. Cf. in ibid, 228–35 the letter referred to from Joseph to Anselmi.
[6]Cf. above, Anselmi to Joseph, 6 August 1937.
[7]Cf. "Spontaneity Is a Form of Organization," Eugenio Colorni's address to the Italian Socialist Party (26–28 June 1937) has not survived.
[8]This is probably the first draft of a project including directives for the work in Italy, attached to "Ruggeri to Joseph," 11 August 1937: cf. below.

you without going through the Erba group. (I have these contacts already through ***, and the comrades in Milan will re-establish them as soon as possible, if they haven't done so already).

From what I've already sent you, you can see that in our view the new Center will have a political rather than organizational function. Its foreign communications will be political in nature — that is, transmission of articles, directives, information and news from us. Information, news, political and cultural press reports in very few copies from you. The recent thing at ***, in this sense, has worked quite well. The new Center should be made up, in the light of recent conversations with Tasca, of L. and myself and P., who would stay temporarily until we can find someone else to bring in, possibly from Turin or Florence or elsewhere. Organizational contacts will have to be through other people, whom we will indicate to you little by little. In any case, be careful to keep the groups in watertight compartments, separated from each other and from the Center. A small example of this practice is the way it has been done at ***, where organizational contact with base leaders has been kept separate from contact with the Center's representative. This has meant that I have been able to assess the situation and issue directives through contact with a single person who knows neither my name nor my address (by the way, be very careful not to let these out, especially not to the *** comrades). In short, you will see that once the initial effort has been made to set up the organizational work on the basis of border centers, things will run smoothly on both the political and practical levels. For the organization and control of the border posts, and for all the Italian work in Paris, you are the only one we can count on, and we therefore sincerely hope that you are in agreement on these projects.

The situation at ***: The letter you sent does not surprise me. The comrades there have always been reluctant about the local newspaper. And if we succeed in setting up a border post we can give up the idea, at least for now, because I will also be busy reorganizing the Center. The news you got from the messenger probably came out of a conversation during an evening of enthusiasm. They probably requested orders from the Center because I only had direct contact with one person from the group, and I didn't identify myself as an actual representative of the Center. At *** a certain activist enthusiasm is widespread in some areas. The environment is a bit untrustworthy, in terms of provocateurs. But the element I've been in contact with — the same one you write to — is a serious person. The only risk is that he might fall into the hands of some provocateur. You can continue to communicate with me by writing to him, calling me A., and without emphasizing that I'm a member of the Center. And write only what is strictly necessary. For example don't repeat the same thing in three separate letters, the way you did before — that I should send out articles and take care of rebuilding the Center. We will take care to acknowledge receipt of every letter that arrives, and you can be sure that everything you write will receive maximum consideration. The address you have for me belongs to people who know nothing of any of this; if the police got suspicious and came to them, they would immediately cough up the name and surname of the person they were passing the letters to. So as you see this is a reason to write only when necessary. I'm done. Best wishes. I'll be here till Friday, so get back to me right away.

Anselmi

5. Letter of Ruggeri to Joseph

The Problem of the Italian Center

11 August 1937

Dear Joseph,

I am answering yours of the 9th, which cheered me because I found substantial agreement between us on the main points. I know your document well — it was the first thing my host gave me when I arrived here. Actually, my plans were not meant to be anything other than a development of your own ideas. I will now try and set out point by point the common elements of your plan and mine and, as you will see, there is substantial agreement and the disagreement is limited to the emphasis on a single point. My plans certainly are schematic, but a framework is always schematic, and obviously I am aware like you that the reality is much more complex than frameworks of this type. Nevertheless, I believe they are very useful for pointing the work in a precise direction.

The problem of the Italian Center: Agree completely on points 3 a, c, and d of your plan. Your objections concerning the uncertainty of relations between my plan's Center and apparatus basically show that the plan is actually not as schematic as you say. I deliberately left this part vague and uncertain, because this is a case where only experience can establish the method to be followed, place by place. The Center must never under any circumstances be an inner sanctum, an academy. It has to have roots that go deep into the situation, it has to represent the mindset and needs of all strata of the Party and know the temperature of the masses. Establishing this kind of contact, this close attachment to the concrete situation is something that each Center representative will have to do alone, according to his own means and temperament and the situation he is in; he will have to set the tempo and the limits. What I wanted to argue is that these contacts have to be *legal* even when they concern organized and active elements. What I mean is that a member of the Center, when communicating with an active element of the base, should not try to delve into the details of the person's work, much less collaborate in it; on the contrary, speaking openly the way one does to a comrade, he should keep the conversation in the realm of overall facts and ideas and the assessment of the situation. It goes without saying that he shouldn't refuse to give the person news, an address or a contact if he needs them and gives sufficient guarantees. I know all this is vague, but it is meant to be. I repeat that it is right to tell members of the Center that they should maintain close contact with the political situation; but it is impossible to give precise instructions that tell them *how*.

I do not agree, however, on point 3b of your plan, which calls for an internal Organizational Center. I'm sure this would quickly end up being identified with the Political Center (which is in fact what happened with the old Center) and the result would be the usual congestion, with all its serious drawbacks.

And today, as you know, there is nobody in Italy with the qualities necessary for the formation of an Organizational Center [. . .]. This is not defeatism. The groups have to do their work. But with limited responsibilities, in watertight compartments, and in direct contact with foreign countries. You yourself, in point 3d, entertain the possibility of foreign border posts. I would emphasize this aspect and abandon point 3b. You *have got to* set up these border posts; otherwise we can't work. My host agrees. You are the best person to do this. The money will be found. We will give you all the information we can find. It is unthinkable that a party headquartered abroad, in contact with the International and all the foreign socialists, one of whom is in power, and which has around 3000 members abroad, can't find five dependable people willing to do a job that would be to their own advantage, both politically and morally as well as materially. Setting up border posts means looking out for the safety of dozens of comrades inside Italy. The Paris office will naturally have an organizational character, and this will be expressed essentially in relations with the border posts — and through these, with Italy. Obviously, until the border posts are working the Paris office will still maintain its direct contacts with Italy. But these will gradually decrease once the border posts are up and running.

I enclose a new outline regarding the responsibilities of the Center, which the party leaders agree with. As you can see, the Center has been left wide latitude and the possibility of exerting decisive influence on decisions concerning our work in Italy. This fits with what you wanted (pages 1 and 3 of your letter of 9).

The work of the cadres and the masses: I agree completely that the work will essentially have to be done by cadres. The thrust of my argument in the article on spontaneity was toward finding a means that would allow cadres to establish contact with the masses while at the same time preserving their position as cadres; and I am glad you agree about this. I fully accept the additions and clarifications you give in n. 4 of your plan. I also mean the thing just the way you set it out.

Internal press: I don't think it's right that the internal press, with the enormous difficulties it brings, should have an ideological character, the way *Echi* did. The ideological work can and should be done in the newspaper. The internal press should be reserved for instant propaganda, for which a delay of even a week could be harmful. The internal press should be contingent in nature, right on top of the situation in a city or a factory. An analysis of the nature of fascism or of general directives does not need to be printed on a mimeograph machine under the constant threat of police interference. Remember that the mimeograph is as a rule what gets our comrades caught (look at the mistrust of the *** comrades), and it should be used only for immediate and urgent local purposes. This is in the category of separation between organizational and ideological work.

Material means: We are in a position to take care of ourselves as regards internal work — but you find the money for the border posts. You cannot under any circumstances abandon this project or offer passive resistance to it. We cannot work on that basis.

Relations with the communists and the struggle within fascist organizations: You know that on this subject I am less skeptical than you are and than the old Center used to be. I think we have to start out with the idea of cooperating as much as possible, while safeguarding our independence. I don't think the struggle inside fascist organizations is as utopian as you think. In any case I want to talk to my comrades in Italy before I take a precise position. After we talk, we will probably put our position down in an article. On the other hand (and this was also the position of the old Center), it is probably pointless and harmful to keep coming back to the problem of cooperation etc. We have already decided to cooperate, and we will try to implement this wherever possible (see also the attached directives). I do not see any absolute contradiction between the legal position and our work as cadres. I mean, for example, that in our leaflets we will incite the workers to stand up for their rights with the unions. I tried to give a practical example of what I mean in the piece on the schools. We should try and promote similar articles for other social strata (employees, workers, students, etc.). A joint press run with the communists for propaganda purposes — why not? Indeed, my ideal would be a periodic propaganda leaflet in every city of with the title: *Popular Front Bulletin*. Keep in mind that today the phrase Popular Front carries immense weight with the masses. In my speech to the Congress I identified two conditions which (if actually put into effect) would guarantee our autonomy in an eventual organic unification: a directorate in Italy (therefore not subject to Muscovite bureaucracy), and a refusal to accept anti-Trotskyist discipline. These are two conditions that, in my opinion, the Italian Communist Party will never accept. But for us they are essential. But again, we will discuss this with our Italian comrades.

I have taken note of your provisions regarding Lugano. I will perhaps pass them on to a friend of ours who will be here shortly, and who will present himself to Zanzi with the password Carloni, and will be called Bianco. His name is Bruno Visentini; he is young and capable and in possession of a passport [. . .]. You and he can work out something for the Brenner frontier (he is also a skier). But avoid the usual review of Italians he could visit. *Do not give him any names* — it isn't necessary. He already has his contacts and has no need to set up others. You and he should try and arrange the introduction of material for the Brenner frontier. And nothing else.

Obviously you will need to have names and addresses of the

representatives of each group. But you must not under any circumstances communicate them to members of other groups, even if you know they are secure or they were presented to you as secure. Give only the names that are necessary. If you know that someone has a contact, there is no reason for you to name him, not even to the Almighty. Excuse my insistence on this point. But I repeat, you have named me, for example, a number of times to people you thought were safe, but who had no reason to know I am active. And now, for example, communist friends have sent word to me that I should be on guard because my name is known everywhere [...].

I don't know if you know this, but the police came last year to my doorkeeper in Milano asking questions about me. My mail from abroad regularly arrives already opened, and for two years I was regularly refused a passport despite having all the necessary permits, military etc. A few days before I left I decided to go to the police chief of ***, showing that I had serious reasons, both family-related and academic (a congress) for going abroad.[9] And the police chief made me wait a day and then gave me the passport. All of which makes me think he gave it to me just to see what I would do. I have been very careful here, and *nobody but Tasca knows I am here*. Anyway, keep in mind that I am under surveillance.

I hope to get the letter you told me about tomorrow. You won't have time to answer this because I'm probably leaving on Friday. I have decided for certain reasons to change my pseudonym again and call myself Ruggeri. I will let it be known right away in ***, where I will be at the end of next week. I will go to Milan around the beginning of September.

Ciao. Affectionately,
Ruggeri

I will sign the articles with random names, different each time. I'll begin with the initals D. 5.

---

[9] To participate in an international philosophy congress on Descartes, Colorni went to Paris in the summer of 1937, where he made contact, for the first time, with the socialist leaders in exile.

Outline of Directives for Italian Work/Activity

A. *Reorganization of Italian activity abroad*:
   1. Political-organizational center in Paris.
   2. Border posts.
   3. Fund for establishing and operating the posts.

B. *Reconstitution of the Italian Center:*
   1. Political — not organizational — character of the Center.
   2. Its composition; comrades from different cities in periodic contact.

C. *Autonomy and responsibilities of the Center:*
   1. Establishing the political line to be followed by organizations in Italy, within the framework of the general policy of the Party as set by the Congress.
   2. Establishing methods and organizational relations between the Italian and Foreign Centers.
   3. Establishing, case by case and site by site, methods of collaboration with the communists, within the framework of the Unity of Action Pact.
   4. Control over ideological activity and political contributions that are sent from Italy from base elements, so that the distinction between the political line of the Center and simple contributions to the discussion is clear.
   5. Collaboration in Party discussions, and the right of any contribution from the Center or authorized by the Center to be published in Party organs, as long as this does not compromise vital interests of the Party of which the Center is unaware.
   6. Discussion on an equal footing with the central organs of the Party of all matters of general internal and foreign politics.

6. Letter of Ruggeri to Joseph

Border Posts

13 August 1937

Dear Joseph,

Your letter arrived and I only have time for a quick word. Your instructions are duly noted. I talked with our German comrade Paul Bernard about the border posts, and he will give you information and assistance concerning the Brenner when you are in Paris. About Yugoslavia, do you know what has become of a certain Adam, who used make trips between Fiume and Sussak?

I reckon that around the end of September we will have worked out the Italian Center directives, and we'll send them to you. Meanwhile I urge you again to work on the border posts, and not to put anyone you meet in contact with any group other than mine.

With affection, your Ruggeri

Annex: Directives for Establishing Border Posts and for the Work Involved

September 1937

Each border post must consist of one responsible person, recruited from among our Party's best local elements, or else from the on-site ranks of the Socialist Party. It would be pointless to go on about the level of commitment this person is expected to offer. It has to be in any case someone *local,* someone who was born in the area and has lived there many years, who has a long-standing association with the inhabitants and possibly a good knowledge of the border situation. It must be someone *absolutely above the suspicion of the Italian and local police.* The person should have a normal occupation which requires a constant local presence but leaves some amount of spare time. The job will be modestly compensated, and the work will require a genuine commitment, rather than being simply something done for us. A tendency to talk or to brag to friends about having been entrusted with this responsibility will result in immediate termination. I would add that the ideal person would be someone who for work-related reasons often travels back and forth across the frontier.

The duties of the position of border trustee would be as follows. Keeping a depository for printed material, which will be sent periodically from Paris, and either delivering such material to Italian personnel who will arrive with proper identification to collect it, or — and this is the main job — locally managing its introduction into the country. This task would engage the abilities of the comrade in question, whose local knowledge and contacts would be put to use to find travelers, smugglers, etc. As a general rule the border trustee should not be the one who brings material across the border, and travel should be limited to making organizational contact with Italian leaders. The job will involve giving the travelers and smugglers addresses that have been previously agreed upon, *which will never, under any circumstances, be those of the comrades in charge in Italian cities,* and making sure that the smugglers and travelers have as little contact as possible with the addressees, limiting themselves to delivering the material. The trustee will maintain personal contact with one or two (at the most) of the leaders in each of the designated Italian cities, corresponding with them using invisible ink, meeting them during any journeys that might be required, and transmitting directives from the Center. The trustee will be personally responsible for their names, addresses and contact information, which he alone should know and never under any circumstances communicate to anyone. In case he should need to be replaced temporarily, he must first obtain explicit authorization from the Paris Directorate. Through his connection with the leaders in the cities, he will maintain contact with the Center and will receive from them articles, decisions and directives to be immediately transmitted to Paris — this in cases where the Center considers this route better than direct contact with Paris. If he notices even minimal surveillance by the local police or the Italian consulate, the border trustee will report this immediately to the Central Station in Paris. He will also be *obliged* to report any case in which, whether by his own or someone else's carelessness, information has been leaked to someone. I must insist on strict Party discipline being applied to the work of the border trustee. He will have to take responsibility for the commitment taken on, and will be sanctioned if the job is done badly; penalties will range from removal from office to exclusion from the Party to, in extreme cases, public condemnation as a dangerous element.

Internal centers: Each city will have to set up one or more organizational centers, to be directed by a very limited number of leaders. These people will be in contact with the border post, from which they will receive directives from the Center. Together with the border post they will organize the job of introducing printed material. Their internal contacts should concern organization more than propaganda. Roughly, these contacts can be set up as follows:

1) Contact with one or more people whose addresses are maximally secure and who will be responsible for receiving printed material.

2) Contact with a limited number of people who have relationships in various workers' environments or among the middle classes, to whom printed material will be delivered for distribution. The leader should not participate personally in this distribution. Eventually the distributor will probably be able to identify who it is that receives the printed material from abroad. This should be avoided if possible, however, so that the address does not come under police suspicion.

3) Contact with people from the Center. This contact will consist mainly of communicating to the person at the Center impressions, ideas, news about the local situation, and so on. The base leader may receive directives from the person he is in contact with at the Center. The most common way, though, would be to receive them from his border post. [...]

The Italian Center

7. Letter of Ruggeri to Joseph[10]

Anti-fascist Alliances

November-December 1937

Dear Joseph,

Thanks for your news and the good wishes. Thanks also for the newspapers and clippings you've been sending regularly — they are of great interest to us. Please keep sending them. Concerning the Popular Front project you sent us a while back, I've already let you know my generally favorable views.[11] Unfortunately, because of a misunderstanding, the project has come to nothing, and therefore I can't spend time examining it nor even send it to Milan; but probably in the meantime you will have been able to communicate directly with Milan. I say again that my opinion is generally very favorable to the project and I do not share at all the concerns expressed in Modigliani's recent articles. On the contrary, I find the articles completely out of line and inappropriate. Those of us here are in favor of a collaboration to the bitter end — which does not yet mean organic unity. To achieve the latter we will have to be extremely cautious and move very slowly. The tone of Dimitroff's last article, which it seems some of you saw as a new turning point, should not in my view be interpreted as such (unless new facts have arrived). To me it seems more like a tactical move aimed at detaching some groups from the leadership of the Second International, which is still very hostile to collaboration. My feeling is that the attitude of the article leaves all roads open for a collaboration like the one we've had up to now, but possibly takes a step back when it comes to organic unity — which shouldn't displease us, since organic unity would make

---
[10] Letter published in AA.VV. (1963), *Documenti inediti dell'archivio Angelo Tasca*, 258–59.
[11] This was a program of the Antifascist Front of November 1937 proposed by the Communist Party to the Socialist Party, the Republican Party and the Justice and Libery Movement (cf. the editorial on the subject, "Fronte popolare e Fronte antifascista" in *Lo Stato operaio*, 1 Dec. 1937). The project, never published, was sent to these groups, who then discussed it, as this letter shows. The Tasca fund also contains variants proposed by Tasca, the Nenni project discussed at the directors' meeting of 27 November 1937, and the counter-project presented by the Justice and Liberty representatives at the meeting of 18 March 1937 at the headquarters of the Voice of the Italians (note by Stefano Merli).

it more difficult for us to safeguard our autonomy.

I will briefly answer my Austrian friends' questions (actually, I imagine you've probably already given them the same answers[12]):

1) since 1934. Has close relations with the Directorate there, but autonomy for directives concerning activity in Italy — this for general directives which the Internal Center collaborates in formulating.

2) of workers, petty bourgeois and intellectuals. Students and intellectuals sometimes have a leadership role; sometimes they make up groups in themselves, without significant contact with the other groups.

3) the workers are in general older and have had different experiences. The intellectuals are generally young.

4) training of cadres, distribution of printed material, drafting of articles that are sometimes printed internally, sometimes abroad; cooperation with the foreign press (of the Party) through ideological and news articles.

5) with the former, close collaboration in the context of the Unity of Action Pact; with the latter, close friendship and more sporadic collaboration, which at this moment we are trying to make more organic.

6) no; the tendency is to use fascist organizations instead.

7) such phenomena have created spontaneous movements among the masses and have sometimes assumed some importance. In general it may be said that in recent years the masses have shown themselves to be more awake (but this would involve a long discussion). This has brought us a greater influx of young intellectuals. Among the masses, on the other hand, it has brought an increase in spontaneity (I have already noted that our cadres among the workers are no longer so young). Our problem at the moment is to take part in this spontaneity, which may become massive from one moment to the next, to lead it and make use of it as a nursery for new leaders.

8) yes. Yes. Yes. Relationships that are often personal and involve pure friendship, which prove on many occasions to be very useful.

9) the collections of our magazines, and various books published abroad.

Best wishes, etc., Ruggeri

---

[12][il Centro socialista interno al Partito socialista austriaco] [The Italian Socialist Center to the Austrian Socialist Party], now in AA.VV. (1963): 257–58.

Part II

1. Letters to Ursula

Systems[13]

December 10, 1936

Pini my love,

Today I read a long and excellent review on Spinosa; and I must say the direction of my work now seems clear and harmonious. What interests me more and more is how a system is born almost without wanting to be — that is, there are various thoughts and theories scattered about, apparently without connection, and gradually, to the degree that they spread, they automatically make up a harmonious whole, as if they had been deduced one from another. More or less like this:

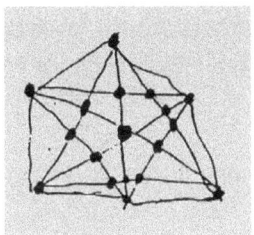

It could be construed that all the points are created according to a rule, as if each had arisen autonomously, like something entirely [illegible] and not taking account of the context. Otherwise, the necessity of the context forces the different points into a wider arrangement. The system comes at the end, like an unexpected gift. But it always comes; and the fact that it infallibly arrives is a problem in itself. Don't read this to Bernd; otherwise he'll think I'm an empiricist, individualist, etc., which I am not.

Your Eugenio

---

[13]Translated from the German into Italian by Giuseppe Franco.

Reading Literature

Trieste, October 4, 1938

My Dearest

I try to take my mind off things reading the books from the prison library — I read a couple of those great historical novels from the last century (Tommaso Grossi, Sienkiewicz), which I hadn't read before, and I was quite disappointed — flat, banal, lacking the most elementary psychology, coarse in every way. Kipling's *Kim*, on the other hand, I liked a lot more. I think he is able to give the story a color and tone that you don't easily forget. I also read Chesterton's *The Man Who Was Thursday*; it's one of those novels that are so common today, like Kafka, all hinging on a gimmick, a transposition of terms between ironic and hallucinatory. I've now managed to get hold of two of Shakespeare's tragedies from the prison library, and I've promised myself to read them very slowly, savoring them word by word — so they'll last longer. But I really miss my books and my work.

Your Eugenio

Reading Shakespeare

Trieste, October 8, 1938

My Ursula,

I'm reading some of Shakespeare's magnificent tragedies. The characters — all monumental, and in so few words! I'm beginning to think that all the greats (Dante, Shakespeare, Goethe) stand out for the few words they use to express themselves — their work is epigraphic and sculptural, and in Goethe it becomes succinct, like a proverb.

Eugenio

Reading Kipling, Turgenev, and Slataper

Trieste, October 12, 1938

My Ursula,

I think what you write about Kipling is absolutely right: just as you say — a world without beginning or end. People who don't know what it means to hurry. And hurrying always includes the sense of finishing, the sense that there is a beginning and an end. I found the same feeling a bit in the short stories of Turgenev I'm reading, collected in *Sketches from a Hunter's Album*. The eastern world has no fear of dying. It stands still, waiting. Time has no value.

I'm also reading *Il mio Carso* by Slataper. I like it quite a lot and I think you would too, because there's a physical, almost sensual feeling for the landscape here around Trieste.

Your Eugenio

Reading Slataper and Ibsen

Trieste, October 15, 1938

My Ursula,

My reading during the last three days has been: *Il mio Carso* by Slataper, and Ibsen's *Hedda Gabler*. The first of these interested me a lot: a man. A being who is passionate about sincerity, someone you would like to have as a friend. He is a born writer — a poet even when he confesses in the most personal and almost immodest way. *Hedda Gabler* impressed me as well. She is one of those female literary figures of the last century who would be, like *Anna Karenina*, *Madam Bovary*, etc., the perfect part for Greta Garbo (or maybe she has already played her?).

Your Eugenio

Reading Schiller and Shakespeare

Trieste, October 17, 1938

My Ursula,

My regular and monotonous everyday life here goes on. I read, from the prison library, Schiller's *Don Carlos* and Shakespeare's *The Tempest*. I liked *Don Carlos* much more than I thought I would. It's a complex tragedy, human and without stereotypes. It's the best thing of Schiller's that I've read (although I've read very little). And *The Tempest* is a delight. It pairs up well with *A Midsummer Night's Dream*, but is perhaps even more beautiful. It's strange how Shakespeare is able to make you feel and breathe an atmosphere and landscape almost without describing it at all. There are almost no descriptions in *The Tempest* — but still the reader experiences the landscape of that island in every minute detail. As you see, I am acquiring literary culture and practicing my critical skills.

As there is nothing else....

Your Eugenio

Reading Shakespeare and D'Azeglio

Trieste, October 25, 1938

My Ursula,

I have read Shakespeare's *Tempest*. It's one of those plays in which genius borders on madness — it's so strange and bewildering, fragrant and mysterious at the same time, tragic and burlesque!

I'm also reading Massimo D'Azeglio's memoirs — one of those books I should have read as a child, but which interests me now because of the environment it describes.

Your Eugenio

Reading Physics and Don Quixote

Varese, December 16, 1938

My dear good Ursula,

I'm getting on with my studies and reading. I would like to read Haas's book on material waves and quantum mechanics in German. But for now I still have a long way to go to finish studying the physics in Perucca's book. I've finally finished *Don Quixote*. It's a fairly entertaining book, but it didn't impress me as the great masterpiece everyone talks about. I think it loses a lot in translation and in Spanish the style must be wonderfully fluid and familiar, like Voltaire and Diderot. The second volume (written ten years after the first) is the best, and it is touching to see how the author's affection for his characters grows and he makes them more and more human and almost melancholy, and less and less clownish.

Your Eugenio

Two Psychological Mechanisms

Trieste, December 20, 1938

Ursula my dearest,

I also know so well and have suffered so much from that condition of being at the mercy of your own thoughts, futile and banal, which you are ashamed of for their mediocrity — of sitting for hours at a desk in front of something that perhaps is good and that interests you, but that you can't seem to focus your mind on. And everybody thinks you are studying and working hard, and perhaps even admires you for it; and you . . . out of the five hours at the desk, you've spent four and a half of them daydreaming about the color of a dress, or singing a little tune to yourself to the rhythm of some noise outside, or imagining in detail a scene where you invent such and such a person and tell him this and that, and he answers such and such, etc.

Not to go on about myself, but just to give you the feeling of this "common ailment" — of how very many of these pointless and mediocre daydreams there are in eight years of work on the philosophy of Leibniz. You say to me: okay, but how can you escape from them, where do you get the willpower? I don't know much either, but I want to say two things:

1. Willpower is one of those words that don't mean anything, or at least not much. The doctor tells the patient "exercise your will," and the patient answers: "But my illness is precisely that I don't know how to exercise my will." The point is to find the psychological mechanism that drives you to want something, that chains you to the desk so that out of the five hours of which four and a half are daydreams, at least half an hour is work. I know of two of these mechanisms and both are artificial. One is social convention. The whole world expects a graduate in philosophy to study, write, etc. The official world of science prepares an environment for him so that what he does, even though devoid of any intrinsic motive, will be valued. But if he can't show that he has spent those five hours at his desk, whatever it was he was doing, no one will take notice of him. No one, on the other hand, expects a woman to spend five hours at a desk. For her public opinion is a deterrent rather than an

incentive. Live in an environment where it's normal for a woman to pursue intellectually productive activity, and the task will be much easier for you. Outside commitments are also useful for this (exams, obligations to present a paper, etc.). 2. The second "mechanism" I know is axiomatic, perhaps even aggressive, self-confidence. That confidence that leads you to latch onto any excuse to believe that what you're doing is important. In the end, those university and literary circles I spoke badly about in one of my recent letters at least have the one benefit of being institutes created to keep you chained for those famous five hours to your desk. O sheet of paper, why can't you be longer?

Your Eugenio

Walt Disney, Childhood, and Imagination

Trieste, December 28, 1938

My Ursula,

I still have a lot to say about the things in your latest letters. You are absolutely right about Walt Disney's films. All he's done is take his cue from the story of Snow White in order to indulge his countless variations on the grotesque theme of the seven dwarfs, which is all he is capable of. Everything in the film apart from the seven dwarfs is flat, thin and banal. The character of Snow White is very weak and the scenes with Prince Charming (or whatever he's called) are truly pitiful. From moving, limpid and rhythmic, as you say, the story has turned into jokes and antics. But that's all he is capable of. Mickey Mouse is basically identical to the seven dwarfs. He's found his formula and he's sticking with it as long as it delivers. But how beautiful the story is, just as you said. And how beautiful it is to understand childhood, and experience your own so intensely. For me, my childhood is a nebulous, dull period with no colors that stand out. A mediocre little boy, a bit cocky, a bit angry, a bit of a liar. For you it was a world of strong feelings and true passions, of dances and rhythms, of falling asleep surrounded by ghosts, of enthusiasm for songs, fairy tales and pictures. Either I don't remember anything of my childhood, or I was nothing more than quiet, well-behaved, best in the class. But I hope our little moppet has a childhood like yours.

And I also want to say something about what you were saying

— whether a child needs impressions that are vivid and varied, or monotone gray (that is, the difference between your childhood and mine — but I think it depends more on nature than upbringing). In any case I wanted to say that this inability to concentrate, this letting yourself be pulled this way and that by your own thoughts is perhaps a female trait, but it is a trait that is essential to intelligence; and it's called imagination. The problem is finding that trick that enables you to channel it and make it productive (and by productive I also mean perhaps only that it gives you joy and a sense of fulfillment). It's almost a question of instinct and flair. You need to be a bit selfish, and have that "organic patience" Goethe talks about — and also, just a bit, you have to know how to say no — that is, how to manage your own capacity to enjoy, and to choose between enjoyments. It's what I would call epicurean asceticism. The danger is "living" always on the edge. You always have to be just a little bit outside yourself, a little bit the spectator, so you'll be able — not very much, I don't say abandon them entirely — but to choose between two daydreams.

Your Eugenio

Analytic Geometry, Imaginary, and Complex Solutions
                                            Naples, January 4, 1939
My Ursula

My study plan for the next months is to continue studying physics from the books of De Broglie etc., to complete my study of mathematics to the extent that I need it to understand physics; and in the meantime to pursue and complete my work on relativity. On this subject, I must say I would have thought there was a way of expressing imaginary and complex numbers in geometric form, for example in analytic geometry. I think such a method could help me understand certain formulas that concern relativity. There is no mention of this in the analytic geometry books but I know there is a method like this, created by Standt (who lived in the last century) and in any case I would like to know his method. I wonder if you might be able to get me some information on this, either by consulting a large general treatise on analytic geometry or asking someone who knows the subject. I don't know if I've explained it well enough. Treatises on common analytic geometry teach that algebraic magnitudes are to be expressed geometrically, in the form of equations. Now these geometric figures generally express the real solutions to these equations. For imaginary and complex solutions (the elementary treatises say), there are no geometric expressions. Now I have read that there are methods (the work of Standt and perhaps others) for expanding the field of analytic geometry so that these imaginary and complex solutions can also be expressed geometrically. And I would be interested to know these methods. The second volume of Bersolari doesn't have them as I had hoped. Who knows if my cultural guide might also become my scientific secretary and set about skimming through library books, the way she did in Berlin for my Leibniz?

Your husband, Eugenio

Popular Poetry

Ventotene, January 21, 1939

Ursula my dearest,

Keep writing to me about your studies and ideas; they interest me very much and make me think. I really like what you write about popular poetry, and I never thought about it in this way — I would like it if you developed this idea and found some examples. There's an essay of Croce's entitled "'Popular' poetry and 'artistic' poetry." I haven't read it, but there might be something in it that would interest you. I also really like the way you write in Italian — you still make some mistakes, but you have a quick and incisive and effective style, I would say almost more effective than in German. Maybe having fewer words at your disposal helps you to be brief and incisive; whereas in a language that is well known one never gets tired of using words to paint shades of nuance and shape concepts. But this is of course a paradox. Anyway, I like the idea of the popular song as an "artistic telegram." I've also been thinking in this period that truly great poetry is almost always an epigraph, a proverb, a quote. Why, I don't know. But the greatest poets (Dante, Shakespeare, Goethe) have all always written in an exceptionally concentrated and epigraphic way. And Shakespeare — he almost gives the impression that he's always in a hurry. Could it be that they have done by themselves what popular poetry has done anonymously and cumulatively? In any case be careful, when you develop these ideas, that you don't formulate them in a way that's too theoretical and conceptual. Take care not to create a "theory" that begins with the question: how shall we define the concept of popular poetry? This is the common defect of the Germans; because in their effort to try to "define the concept," they end up losing the entire essence of their research. Do something instead that's less precise but with lots of examples and lots of concrete observations, without the pretense of wanting to tie everything together in "concepts." And you'll see that it will turn out well and be perfectly suited to your means.

Your Eugenio

Physical Conditions and Mathematics

Ventotene, January 25, 1939

My dearest Ursula,

I'm feeling better, but I'm afraid I'm still far from being really well because I still feel that my nerves are shaky and unable to handle any intellectual effort. Today I'm also a bit tired, because last night I stayed up very late reading the novel *The Stars Look Down*, which is really beautiful, perhaps the best contemporary novel I've read. You also write that you're often tired, and I assure you, the only medicine is to go to bed early. I read a little now (novels) and always think a little about the theory of imaginary numbers — but really without pushing myself, only when I feel like it, and only until I get tired. I wish I had a manual job, but here it's not easy to find one. Tomorrow I'm again waiting tables in the mess hall, but it's not a great job. And I have to say that even physically this inner nervous agitation makes me a bit weak. My usual nervous tics always come back out when I'm down, and I can't seem to get rid of them.

Many thanks for the excerpt from the encyclopedia article on Standt, which is very interesting. What I seem to get is that his method is very different from mine; but this is exactly why I would be interested to get to know him, so I could compare it with mine. Maybe you can find something in a specialized mathematics dictionary, or in a history of mathematics (for example that big one of Cantor's).

And in general I would like to know if, even apart from Standt, there are ways of expressing imaginary numbers geometrically.

Your Eugenio

Anthropomorphism, Alternative Views, and Animals

Ventotene, February 3, 1939

And with that we move on to the items on the agenda.

Which begin, my darling, with the first point in the discussion you had with Silvia on the business about the ant and about eating meat, in which your answer was right and correct in the sense I intended. Obviously, when I talked about an ant's point of view compared to a human's, I said "ant" just to give a random example. I could have said any other thing: a microbe, a vegetable; any hypothetical point of view from which the things in the world could be organized in a way different from the way a person does it. This has nothing to do with saying that an ant "is worth more" or less or the same as a person. This anthropomorphic way of thinking about things from the point of view of "being worth more, or less" strikes me as one of the main features of Silvia and Willy's way of thinking. They apply the criteria of "good" and "bad" to everything, to ants and people, horses and microbes, luminous vibrations and universal gravitation. It's a typical example of this desire to put ourselves and our own standards of human judgment at the center of everything; this wanting to transpose concepts that are valid for us and in a certain area of our lives, as if they could be universally valid in all fields. When I speak of the possibility of other points of view and ways of organizing what we call reality, I do not at all mean to limit such ways to the animal kingdom, and I do not mean to say that such ways are more or less valid than ours. They are valid for those for whom they are useful, just as ours are for us. Obviously Silvia must have reported our discussion of this summer to some friend of yours, who must have misunderstood it and taken it for a discussion about whether animals have souls — an argument as old as philosophy itself. To resolve this argument you would need to: 1) Come to a clear agreement on what we mean by "soul"; and right there you would be stuck forever. 2) You would need to know animals from the inside, the way we know ourselves; and this for us is impossible. Looking at the big picture and judging from outward appearances and from our own way of organizing things, I think you could say that the animal world is organized according to forms and categories that follow a progression from the so-called lower animals to man, without breaks. But we mustn't forget that even this organization is devised by humans, following human methods and purposes; and it can't therefore be given an absolute value. I was just reading in Enriques' book *The Problem of Life*, that the study of anthropomorphic apes has made many biologists abandon the concept of a clear separation between animals and man. As for eating meat from animals, it is undeniable that we feel greater repugnance at killing or eating a creature the more closely it resembles us; and that in the case of an ape for example, even if its flesh were good, we would probably eat it unwillingly. But abstaining completely from eating meat would definitely involve an expenditure of attention and energy that would divert attention from other tasks concerning people, not animals. In conclusion, people's moral sympathy is attracted by other beings the more they are or seem like us. The wish to bring all animals into the sphere of your own moral sympathy (of which the precept "thou shalt not kill" is an expression) seems today a bit premature. Read my ravings to Silvia if you like. Well then, my impertinent lady wife, I say to you that your husband feels fine and feels his strength coming back.

Your Eugenio

Imaginary Numbers and Analytical Geometry
                                        Ventotene, February 6, 1939

My dearest Ursula,

Since yesterday the weather here has been marvellous, with sky and sun and sea like you've never seen. I'm fine and in a good mood, and I go walking in the sun, and I don't study much — I mean I don't read much because I do still get tired, but my work on imaginary numbers is effortless and going along smoothly. It consists of going back through analytic geometry and introducing this expression of imaginary numbers; so along the way I'm also studying analytic geometry. I think it might be quite interesting, but it's probably already been done. Anyway, now that the principles are in place, their application is easy and enjoyable. Tell me your idea about psychology. Right now I can think only if you give me the inspiration.

Your Eugenio

Trieste and Confined Fellows

Ventotene, February 10, 1939

My darling Ursula,

You know, a Triestine internee has just now come into the dormitory singing:

Mein lieber Augustin
indò ti va coll'ombrellin?
in der Luft in der Luft senza paprika
vado in un giardin.

[My dear Augustin
where are you going with your umbrella?
in the air in the air without paprika
I'm going into a garden.]

Do you like it? In the dorm we are all Triestines or semi-Triestines — that is, one real Triestine, one Dalmatian, one Capodistrian, and me. My darling, just now there was roll call and I answered it and now I'm back to writing to you while the others are making their beds. You can't imagine how nice it is for me to be with Triestines. All the stories we tell each other are about Trieste, about the streets and cafes and restaurants — all places I've been with you, and I feel transported back into that world where we spent our most beautiful years. But we'll have many, many more beautiful years, won't we my darling? And we're still very young and we have lots of years ahead of us.

Your Eugenio

Jokes and Books

Ventotene, February 18, 1939

My Ursula,

Today I took the jar of jam you sent me into the mess hall, and I politely offered it to my fellow diners. But I had filled it with that laundry detergent that looks like jam. Now the barber, who was one of the victims of the joke, has promised to make me eat soap when he shaves me. We'll just see if he can. The dentist is here for two weeks and I'm having two teeth filled, for 50 lire. I still have around 400 lire; in a while I will ask you to resupply me.

Thanks for the index from Standt. I understand perfectly what it's about — they're all topics already dealt with at the beginning of the Bersolari book, which I have here. So you needn't bother with it further. If you're getting books from Trieste, please also send: Castelnuovo, *Analytic Geometry* (1st volume), Vivanti, *Infinitesimal geometry, with related exercises* (3 volumes). I'll send you a list of the books I want in my next letter.

Your Eugenio

Reading Nietzsche

Ventotene, April 4, 1939, evening

My dearest Pini,

Yesterday and the day before I did a big cleanup job on my room, I beat the mattress and covers and put them out in the sun, and I put new paper on the table and shelves. Today I waited tables, and towards evening I started studying. Everything I wanted to write myself has already been written by a certain Nietzsche in his book *Beyond Good and Evil*. I leave you now to plunge into reading it, and if the mood strikes me, to begin the first section of my essay.

Your Eugenio

Mozart and "The Philosophical Illness"

April 5, 1939, evening

My Pini,

I'm in my room and I have the window open. Across the square I hear a gramophone and radio playing Mozart's "Kleine Nachtmusik." It's the first piece of classical music I've heard in seven months. This evening I got your telegram of safe arrival from Milan. I have in front of me the first page of the "philosophical illness." During the day I studied the theory of relativity for a bit. Now my roommates are calling me to play "Don't get angry." On my way I shall pack my pipe with your excellent tobacco.

Your Eugenio

Multiple Undertakings

April 6, 1939, afternoon

I'm feeling fine and happy, but a little disheveled. I'm letting myself do whatever I want to do in the moment. One moment I study physics, then geometry, then I read a novel, then Nietzsche, then I write a page, then I stretch out and think of you. And so on the whole I don't finish anything. But it doesn't matter; I've got out of the habit of set programs — so many pages a day, so many hours at my desk.

Your Eugenio

Birds and "The Philosophical Illness"

Ventotene, April 24, 1939

Pini my dearest,

I'm now working at full capacity, and I'm happy with what I'm doing. The weather is magnificent. All the swallows are arriving now, along with the other birds from the coast of Africa. They're so tired when they get here that the kids can hit them with rocks or even catch them in their hands, and then they sell them for a few cents. So lots of people make meals of stewed birds — they're very good, but I'm so tender-hearted I can't bring myself to eat them — it puts me off to see them whole with their heads and everything. Because they're tiny and you eat them in one bite, bones and all.

My "philosophical illness" is moving along slowly. It's in semi-autobiographical form, but I only isolate facts that can help explain the "philosophical illness." But in a few pages I'll move on to actual philosophy.

Eugenio

"The Philosophical Illness"

Ventotene, April 26, 1939

Ursel my dearest,

I couldn't sleep last night, to the great advantage of my essay on the "philosophical illness," which grew by several pages. It ought to be finished, I think, in 15 to 20 days. I don't want to make predictions, out of superstition.

Your Eugenio

Books of Physics and Psychology

Ventotene, April 27, 1939

My Ursula,

Good for you for getting the Vassler book — he is a highly regarded critic here in Italy as well. So if your Mom has the occasion to buy books, she could get me Planck's *Theoretical Physics,* and Born's book on relativity, and maybe some books by the psychologists Adler and Jung, who interest me on account of the "philosophical illness."

Eugenio

Studying Physics

Ventotene, undated

My Pini,

The sun is beautiful today, and this morning I did gymnastics for two hours; so I feel good and I've lost a little weight. Then I studied physics for a while, which is pretty boring. I really need to make up my mind to let my actual work go for a bit, and get down to filling the gaps I have in the area of science. But it's a pretty boring job.

Eugenio

"The Philosophical Illness" and Reading Nietzsche and Thomas Mann

Ventotene, May 1, 1939

My dearest,

I am fine, and getting on with working. The first chapter of my semi-philosophical piece is almost done, and I feel quite good about it. I've had to let the mathematics go a bit, but I'll get back to it soon. Now and then I also still read Nietzsche, the only philosophy writer I'm able to read just now; and I think this is the basic difference between a person affected by the philosophical illness and someone who has recovered from it — whether or not they can read Nietzsche. (In fact philosophers look down on him as a non-philosopher). I don't know if you get what I'm saying — Nietzsche is much harder to read than Kant. Because the effort you make to read him has to be renewed on every page, and there isn't the sort of coherence that grabs you and pulls you out of your laziness. But one accusation and objection can be applied to him, which I will express in his own words: "Der Liebhaber der Erkenntnis soll seine Ohren überhaupt dort haben, wo ohne Entrüstung geredet wird. Niemand lügt so viel wie der Entrüstete."[14] Then I'll tell you something Bradley said that I read in the philosophy book you sent me: Metaphysics consists of looking for bad reasons to support what we believe by instinct. And I tell you — I'm afraid I'm just too lowbrow to understand Th. Mann. I will explain (I assure you this is not a pose): your position here sounds superficial to my ears. You still don't understand anything. What I mean is that everything he writes, he writes with the idea that it should be rooted, you might say, in something intimate, something deep, something intangible; which out of good taste, an exquisite sense of proportion and a certain modesty, he never expresses openly and aggressively, content instead to leave this something to those able to get it. Now, I am still not able to; my ears are still too tough. I can understand these things if someone tells me them in plain and simple black and white, the way Proust does, for example. But to feel them as a hidden world boiling under the flat, heavy prose of the stories of Joseph, is for me too much work.

---

[14] "The lover of knowledge should in any case put his ears in a place where there is no indignant talk. No one lies so much as someone who is indignant."

But still, having understood this is in itself a start at throwing off my uncouthness. And I came to this while writing the philosophical illness, where it seemed ugly even to me to say things in such a garishly open way. But I have to recognize that there is something unhealthy, "tentative" I would say, about his style, which is so apparently honest and clean. I know from experience what a terrible illness it is to be committed to being "complete," to not leaving anything out. Maybe I can't put up with it because it's the same illness I have (the philosophical illness). And the way I know he has it is from one simple fact — that the novel was supposed to appear in two volumes (or three); four have already come out and it still isn't finished. This, my dear, is fear, fear of not having been honest or complete enough — it is a pang of conscience, a sense of guilt that won't leave you in peace. Tell me if you understand this. In the "philosophical illness" I should also write about you. I don't do so out of modesty, no, jealousy.

Eugenio

The German Language, Not Submitting to It
Ventotene, May 6, 1939

My dearest Pini,

Please, in your next letter don't forget Hölderlin's poetry. Where neither he nor Kleist, nor Nietzsche succeeded (all three of them went mad), George did. That's why I like him. Certainly you get the impression that this battle against the language completely exhausted him and that he didn't do anything else; and in his writings you sense the effort the victory cost him. But in Thomas Mann, I would say, there is too much resignation — the interminable alleyways he takes to reach his destination, seeing that the main road is blocked. It's almost an affectation. "Der Deutsche," Nietzsche writes, "ist beinahe des *Presto* in seiner Sprache unfähig."[15] This means that for someone who thinks at a "presto" tempo, the language in itself is a problem. But it also means that "style" — valuing language in itself, that is — is only to be found in those madmen who racked their brains trying to remake language the way they wanted it. In the

---

[15] "The German is almost incapable of *presto* in his language."

others, including Goethe (and Nietzsche says this as well) you get the impression that the language dominated them. Now I can assure you that letting yourself be dominated by language, as did Goethe and Mann, is exactly analogous to letting yourself be dominated by the philosophical illness — to say something you've thought of, you set out at a comfortable trot, and "prove it" from top to bottom over the course of four hundred pages without skipping anything, so as to be armored against any assault. This (you recognize every step of the journey) is fear. It is the need for armor, for a defense. In conclusion, I will let you love your language, on the condition that you love it like Hölderlin and Nietzsche and George — in order to do it violence; not like Goethe and Mann, to submit to it. Please keep writing to me on this subject, because I'm openly stealing from you a chapter for my book, entitled "the deceit of words." And don't complain, because if you want to write these same things yourself it's fine, you still can — the two of us will always write so differently that we will always end up saying different things. In the meantime I will say that the Italian in your letter on Hölderlin was magnificent, lively, concise, perfect. And now the roll-call has rung.

Ciao, my sweethearts — all three. Eat a lot, all three of you.

A hug from your Eugenio

Psychology

Ventotene, 29 May 1939

My darling,

Now I want to answer Willy's argument, that what psychology always deals with is thought, and therefore thought "exists" before psychology. The initial response is to laugh, and then not to answer. It's an argument that doesn't interest me and tells me nothing, because I don't know what it might mean to say that "thought exists" and "psychology exists." The second response (if you really want to respond) is that it is not true that it is thought that psychology deals with. It is sympathy and antipathy, love and hate, the eyes, the hands, gestures; it is the intonation of the voice, and the "personal intonation" that lies behind every word. All this is what psychology does, and not "thought" — that thing that is so small-minded and pretentious that it says "cogito ergo sum," and speaks in subjects and predicates, and formulates judgments and syllogisms, deluding itself that in this way it has exhausted all the possible manipulations man is capable of, when actually all it has done is express one of them, and in a way that is very approximate and is susceptible to the most disparate and contradictory interpretations. The way I see it, a glance, a hand gesture, a kiss, a slap, all have a demonstrative value (and I insist on this word) just as great as reasoning. Now maybe Willy will be able to prove to you that even a glance and a kiss are "thought." I don't know; if it is true, as Silvia writes, that he is nauseated by arguments and proofs, it seems to me he should be nauseated by thought; just as, honestly, I am as well.

Your Eugenio

Dialectics and Great Philosophers

Ventotene, June 5, 1939

Pini my dearest,

Just now you must be on your way to Venice, and I can't wait to hear that you have arrived. Yesterday I had nothing from you. I'm hoping for tomorrow, so please send me a wire as soon as you've done the exam. I would like to write you something helpful for the exam, but I don't know what, because I'm also so far removed from that way of thinking right now. About Fichte, Schelling and Hegel, it seems to me the most important thing is the concept of the dialectic, which represents a real discovery and a liberation from preconceived frameworks. It means, basically, that what we consider to be "reality," to be an "object," is not that in and of itself, but only because we consider it to be, only because we stand before it as before something external to us, acting on us. The concept of the dialectic basically means that the ideas of subject and object, of "me" and "outside of me," are not absolute, but are only relational tools we need to get our bearings. In this sense, the concept of the dialectic has carried forward the inversion of values that began with Kant, saying that all categories — space, time, substance, causality, etc. are not reality in themselves, but our ways of seeing things. The harm Hegel did was to make these discoveries into a myth and, instead of interpreting them as a useful tool for the development of science and knowledge, to devise a sort of world history for which this dialectic would be the mainspring. This type of philosophy is a typical example of the process by which an "instrumental" idea becomes "substantial." Such "substantializing" characterizes all western philosophy, starting with Plato.

About Descartes, to understand him you have to remember this — that he was infatuated with the geometric method of Galileo's that had worked such wonders in physics; and that he realized that in order to introduce this method in the schools, replacing scholastic-Thomistic physics, you would have to be able to use the method to prove all the axioms of metaphysics and the dogmas of religion, beginning with the existence of God and the immortality of the soul. So to do this he brings in a geometric metaphysics, based on math-style syllogistic reasoning and drawing on the vast field of scholasticism itself (Ontological proof of the existence of God, etc.).

Leibniz: The one thing that impresses him most of all is the causal connection of all things with each other. From any occurrence, through a chain of cause-and-effect links, you can go back to any other occurrence. This means that from anything that happens you can go back into the past and come back into the future, so you can start from any occurrence and describe the world. The world, described taking any fact as a starting point, is the monad. Therefore there are infinite monads, all different (because each has a different starting point) but all representing the same world. (This is the pre-established harmony among the monads).

Remember that your professor leans toward positivism. Therefore you will please him if you tell him this original idea of mine: That the idealist proof that nothing exists beyond the spirit has the same logical structure as the ontological proof of the existence of God. In both cases a deduction about reality is drawn from a logical contradiction. Both are based on the tacit presumption that logic is real.

I have to run and set up. A big hug.

Your Eugenio

Philosophies and Coherence

Ventotene, June 7, 1939

Pini my dearest,

Now I'll answer your philosophy questions. First of all I don't like what you write at all — that you're about to fully embrace the methods of modern psychology. Remember that "fully embrace" is what people do only if they have no ideas. Intelligent people like you don't "fully embrace." They extract, they admire, they become infatuated perhaps, but always with that superiority that makes you master of the instrument, not its slave. Actually, this criticism is superfluous, since I know that you will never "fully" embrace anything, but I wanted to offer it anyway, because it helps me answer your question on "concentric circles." The answer is this — that the philosophical disease is harder to eradicate than you might think, and that it lurks in the most unimaginable places and people — for example, even in my wife, when she stops being a simple receiver and detector of waves (which is already beautiful), and starts to get involved in building something. All these concentric explanations are in fact "philosophies." Each coherent in itself, each "true" from a certain point of view, each "beautiful," "satisfying," "habitable"; sometimes "exciting." Because philosophies are indeed made to be "satisfying," "calming," to explain coherently. No wonder, then, if they turn out to be satisfying, calming and coherent. Now just take each of these concentric circles and ask yourself — what good are they beyond giving me all this satisfaction? And then you will see all this beautiful concentricity and coherence fall apart, and each of the circles will prove no longer to be a self-contained whole, but something detached and fragmentary. The utility of the dialectic is in interpreting some spiritual things and some historical phenomena, and that's all — it's not good for anything else. Analytic psychology is useful in treating certain nervous disorders, and helping us understand certain mental processes even in healthy people, and that's all — it's not good for anything else. Kant helps physics deal with time and space and causality his way. And he's not good for anything else. You ask me if it also makes me nervous to see how easily our minds think in analogies, which we then take to be facts. Does it make me nervous! I've been nervous for twelve years, and only now have I begun to sort this out.

I like the fact that you have also felt this pull toward "coherence," and then you immediately got suspicious. The pull is of course philosophy. People who are passive and just "let themselves live" may be immune to it. But anyone who wants to construct, think about and control their own actions seldom escapes the net. The difficult thing, the exciting thing, is precisely this being able to build and control, while resisting all the magnets that continually pull you towards some "coherence" or other.

When you get this letter it will be the day of the exam. Break a leg. And wire me as soon as it's over. I'll cross my fingers. Ciao, and sorry about the nasty letter and my bad mood of a few days ago.

Your Eugenio

Physics, St. Augustin, and St. Thomas

Ventotene, June 8, 1939

Pini my dearest,

My studies are a disaster, because I can't ever seem to get down to a routine covering all the topics of physics and mathematics; and I'm always getting new ideas. What I should have is a period of quarantine, so I can finish my preparation. I've now let philosophy go a bit, and I'm totally immersed in physics, where I feel I've made some progress. On the question of St. Augustine and St. Thomas you are absolutely right. Besides which, Silvia must have spoken from hearsay, because she certainly hasn't read St. Augustine, and even if she's read a few pages of St. Thomas, he is so difficult and complicated and philosophical, she won't have understood a thing. And with that, bye bye sweetheart, good luck with the philosophy, and the German writing, if this arrives after the philosophy exam.

Your Eugenio

Nervous Diseases Induced by Parents, in Psychology and Literature
Ventotene, June 10, 1939

Dear colleague,[16]

I can't wait any longer to answer you about your idea of destiny as guilt, which is beautiful. First of all, I'll bet you a beautiful gift that you won't pursue this project, by which I mean I'll give you a huge and beautiful gift if you do. In the second place, the topic is so vast that it can also be applied in other fields (in pedagogy, for example). Third — I'm the first to recognize that the topic belongs entirely to you, so if you don't do it no one else will. And now for the argument (the comment, that is, because I agree with it completely). It is true that in modern psychology there is a certain "innatism" that in some ways clashes with and goes against the entirely concrete and empirical tone of this science. "Complexes," developments during childhood, are a given — a fated and inevitable development. At the same time it is clear that they happen by "induction" on the part of the parents. And this explains the inheritance of anxiety; I believe that most nervous diseases are not really inherited, but "induced" (the word that seems to fit the case best) by parents who, even out of love for their children, let themselves be drawn into "identification"; into satisfying instincts and feelings of their own, that is, that their children don't know the least thing about — I mean, essentially, that in loving their children, they think more about themselves than the children. (And I am increasingly convinced that true love consists of this: making the beloved object "exist"). Once the mechanism of this process is known, the Oedipus complex ceases to be an obligatory development, becoming instead malleable, moldable at will. In this way it is possible to think seriously about "manufacturing" the human character and supplying it with whatever psychic qualities we want, following a recipe. Now, when it comes to literary interpretation, certainly for the Greeks (that is to say, Sophocles) this was already so deeply rooted that they could not get rid of it — but they had dark suspicions about their own origins along with a mixture of veneration and resentment for the authors of their misfortunes. This sense of ambiguity the Greeks had toward their gods (so humanly similar to their parents) is something worth highlighting (and the

---

[16]Ursula had just received her university degree.

critics have not done so at all). For us, the more we lose our sense of the family origins of our anxieties, the more our idea of God distances itself from our parents — the more, that is, our consciousness becomes logical and rational. But I repeat — over and above literary interpretation, it seems to me that this idea is fruitful in the sense that it allows the Oedipus complex to be manipulated as an instrument. And here again, progress occurs when something loses its static fixity as a "law of nature" and becomes an instrument in our hands. I think I have something that I wrote some time ago on this issue among my papers. If you're interested I'll look for it and send it to you.

Your Eugenio

Hegel and Dialectical Unrest

Ventotene, June 14, 1939

Pini my dearest,

Since last night I've been racking my brains over your diagram of Hegelian phenomenology, and I don't understand it at all. And what's worse, I'm not the least bit interested in understanding it. There's only one point that's clear — what you say about the possibility of developing a thesis on the concept of the dialectic intended as "restlessness of the object." It seems to me, though, that you are being one-sided here, because the concept of dialectical unrest cannot refer only to the object; it has to apply equally to the subject. Subject and object, in Hegelian philosophy, are one, and therefore must always be united.

Eugenio

Tiredness, Loneliness, and Hard Work

Ventotene, June 24, 1939

Pini my dearest,

I find myself in a curious state. My head is so full of scientific developments and study ideas that I don't know where to start and I feel tired and weighed down. Now I'm going to take another packet of fitina (the fourth since January); but I think your arrival will be very good for me, because my solitude at the moment forces me to

exercise my brain continuously on scientific matters, and this tires me out. The fact is, I've been working like a madman for two years without any interruption, even in prison. And also my feelings and worries have perhaps worn me down a bit. So you will be my holiday.
Your Eugenio

My Few Intelligent Ideas

Ventotene, June 26, 1939

My sweetheart, I'm afraid that when you get here you will find me too stupid, after all your studies and successes. I never have more than two or three intelligent ideas, and I just go round and round between them until I've worn them out. But when you come I just want to listen to you.
Eugenio

Hoping in a More Relaxed Work

Ventotene, June 29, 1939

My dear Urselchen,
I've been working a lot, and getting results. When you get here I expect to have almost finished this "episode" of ideas and developments, and that way my work will be calmer and more relaxed, so it won't always be on my mind; and also I need some "ideas" and general concepts, after this last month's surfeit of mathematics and physics.
Eugenio

Reading Huxley

Ventotene, December 11, 1939

My Pini,
I've started reading *Mariages,* quite good right from the beginning, *The Good Earth* and Huxley's *Counterpoint,* which I would like to finish; I'm saying, as you see, that I feel able to read.
Eugenio

Breathing Your Same Air

Ventotene, December 12, 1939

Pinchen,

I'm reading *Mariages,* a mediocre novel with the usual types and the usual situations, but recounted, I must say, with a certain verve. But as always, reading a novel makes me think of you, and of us; I can't say exactly how. I would say that right now I don't need so much to talk to you as to be near you, to breathe the same air. And I get a feeling of nausea and suffocation every time we have to be apart. Between us there is nothing, or very little, of what there is in the husbands and wives in the novel — thinking of the other as an "other"; the reticence, saying some things and not saying others.

Eugenio

Rhetoric of Peasant Life and Paradoxes

Ventotene, December 14, 1939

My wife and friend,

I've read *The Good Earth,* a mediocre book in every way, and it makes me angry, this taking advantage of the sentimentality of most readers to make a book a big success. It's just as I imagined it from the title and from the people who like it — just the way I was hoping it wouldn't be. And it's not at all true that it displays a deep understanding of the Chinese soul — you find the same tone in every book that has peasants for protagonists, whether Chinese or Sicilian, or Scandinavian; apart from some local practices and customs — not talking much, that way of treating women, the slow, rapturous tone. These are very easy things to do and, especially mixed with a little rhetoric about the good and fertile land that humans cannot break free of, etc., they have a guaranteed effect on the majority of the public. Note that I am the last to deny that agricultural life has its merits, and a depth and variety that we city dwellers would do well to take in. But this unctuous and rhetorical way of glorifying it makes it unpleasant to me rather than attractive. When will somebody write a book on peasant life that doesn't carry on about the myth of the land, about the man who falls asleep amid the furrows breathing the air of the ploughed clods, who picks up a handful of earth and shouts at his children: don't leave here, because this place is your life? Only then will we begin really to understand what agricultural life is, its beauties and its novelty. After that, reading *Counterpoint* is truly refreshing. It is not a book of paradoxes. It is a very serious book, very deeply experienced. You absolutely must read it. What is a paradox? It is that part of truth that is not commonly expressed. Stating it on its own makes it seem exaggerated and "paradoxical." But it is stated on its own like this precisely because it's the only part that's still worth saying, since the rest is known already by everybody. Every truly intelligent person invents very few things that are new and important as compared with those that already exist. If he talks only about the things he has invented and doesn't remind us that they have to be put in with the many other things that are already known, he is called paradoxical. But this is no reason not to be interested in what he says. Quite the contrary.

Always thinking of you and chatting with you, your friend,
Your Eugenio

Reading Lawrence

Ventotene, December 18, 1939

My Pini,

I had a great day yesterday — I felt really good and I began to work a bit writing my philosophy piece. Today though, I'm a bit down; but it's not really important, because in general I'm doing better. I'm reading a book of Huxley's essays, and Lawrence's *Sons and Lovers*. When I feel a bit more in the mood I'll write more. But today I'm feeling lethargic.

Eugenio

Author's Self-indulgence

Ventotene, December 25, 1939

Pini my darling,

I'm reading Lawrence's *Sons and Lovers,* which is a good book overall — but it always amazes me, in these autobiographical books, when authors speak so well of themselves. Aren't they embarrassed?

Can't they view themselves with a bit of distance? The author's own defects are always so likeable.

There are two authors who manage to find themselves disagreeable and see themselves ironically: Huxley and me. And with that I will take the liberty of reminding you that I am and will always be your devoted and affectionate and loving

Eugenio

Lawrence's Sons and Lovers

December 30, 1939

I've finished Lawrence's *Sons and Lovers,* a very interesting autobiography that explains a lot of things. It tells how he was so tied to his mother that he was not able really to love any other woman; and there's the very interesting story of his painful love for a girl, which he resisted inside himself. You can see that the book was written with no control, and is more interesting as a document than as art. But this is exactly what I like about it. There's a sort of untidiness about the scenes and descriptions that make you feel that he's setting them out just as they happened, without "constructing" them in the least. But reading this book casts a new light on his other book — and you realize that what he presents there as a spontaneous account, the immediacy of actual experience, was for him nothing more than liberation from a nightmare, his joy at the fall of certain inhibitions that had earlier tormented him.

Then I read *School for Wives,* which disappointed me. The treatment of the theme is perfunctory and heavy handed. I think you would be able to do it ten times better. There are extremely astute and profound observations that could be made (that you, from your own experience [and I'm being serious] would be able to make); and instead his observations are just coarse and banal. The only scene that comes to life is the one with the mother and daughter.

Bye then; I know I'm a bit like that husband. But with this difference — you can always tell me about it and, even though maybe not right away, in the long run I'll end up catching on.

Always love

Your Eugenio

Two Types of Novelists

Ventotene, January 4, 1940

My dear friend,

So, the thought for the day is this — that novelists can be divided into two types: 1) Those who need to express things symbolically and set the scene in abstract, unreal worlds. They have one bright idea and then press ahead with that as key — among these I would put Kafka, Chesterton, Pirandello, Molnar (in the *Legend of Liliom*), and the American, Steinbeck, whose little book I read — *Of Mice and Men* — quite moving, but entirely built around a very simple device. Among the painters I would include the surrealists (in contrast to Van Gogh and Cézanne, who are another thing altogether). Among the musicians, Stravinsky. Their originality lies in saying ordinary things in strange ways. This is why they attract, but in the long run they don't last. 2) The others, who have the simple ability to express and photograph their world of ideas. And then the point is to see if their world of ideas is alive, interesting and new, or not. For example, with your permission, the world of Gerhardt Hauptmann is nauseating. I had to give up on the book, fed up with being told that a transatlantic liner is a colossus dominating the elements, and tired of his talk about the intimate chaos that oppresses modern man, caught in the vortex of mechanical civilization. The main character miraculously escapes a shipwreck, and the moment he is brought, still dripping, aboard the rescue ship he wonders, "To what end have our lives been spared?" This is someone who needs to be punched. It's that empty and rhetorical pseudo-profundity of the professional and the merchant, of Mr. average. Plus which, the book is forty years old. But as you said, even now his brothers are easily recognizable scions of fashion. The present analogue of Hauptmann I would say is Wassermann. In a certain way it's amusing to read hugely successful books, to have an idea of public tastes.

Your Eugenio

Need for Irony in Literature

Ventotene, January 8, 1940

My dear Pini,

Your husband has read another book of Huxley's, *Chrome Yellow*, and now wants to attack Anatole France. Most recent thought: great rage against the German novelists, who are utterly devoid of irony. Even the stylized ones I was talking to you about in the last letter in general go about their business in a tone that is a bit strange, between the charlatan and the humorist (think of Picasso, Chesterton, the futurists, etc.); there is a certain posing as original types that they do that makes you think they don't take what they do completely seriously. A Kafka, no — he needs to present himself as a near saint, a martyr, the victim of his artistic demons; he never smiles; he is tragic, lugubrious, infatuated with his work. He takes it so seriously that one day he will die, crushed by it. To me this is horrible. Not because it might be a contradiction in one who is serious, but because we are not permitted to take his own pose seriously. Someone who is truly serious doesn't really need to shout about it and adopt these obsessive attitudes. Out of all the theories of art as contemplation and objectification, the only thing that stays with me is this: a certain calm and sobriety, and if we are saying symbolic and stylized things, a certain irony. But it's still better not to say things that are symbolic and stylized. Many more things can be said speaking in a direct way; and these symbolists — I always get the feeling that they somehow have to hide what little they have to say. Among them, I'm sorry to tell you, I include Th. Mann, who in order to talk about modern man, needs to symbolize him using figures from the Bible.

Your Eugenio

Assimilation of Classics in Our Culture

Ventotene, January 11, 1940

My friend,

I'm now trying to read Anatole France, without much success; he's a spirit we know by heart and who hasn't got much left to tell us. But probably what we know by heart is what he taught us. And with that I will move directly to the next philosophical thought: The scientists of antiquity, even the greatest of them — no one reads them anymore. And why is this? Because by now they have been incorporated into our consciousness. Now this is true, in the end, even for artists, or at least for people of taste and culture. Why do I no longer need to read Anatole France? Because I have already absorbed his revelations about taste and culture just breathing the air of my era — because his contribution is already completely dissolved into my culture. The result is this paradox — the more influence an author has in his own time and the more his teachings have been heeded, the less posterity will need to read him. We remember such authors with gratitude, the way we remember Galileo and Newton, whose original works, however, no one reads — not even scientists.

And so which of the classics should we read, in that case? Those that for some particular reason were not assimilated by history and taste, and which therefore still have something to say to us — that is, those that have been forgotten and are not called classics. Or those that have only formal value and are appreciated only for "how" they said things — but even this "how," the "style," easily becomes a common heritage.

This, I would say, offers artists a lesson in modesty. In the place of the ambition to create something immortal that will endure over the centuries, the ambition to say something new, something that will be so well assimilated in their own time that reading the original work will become superfluous, remembered only with a debt of gratitude.

Your Eugenio

Re-reading Certain Classics

Ventotene, January 18, 1940

Pini my dear,

I'm reading another book of Steinbeck's, *Tortilla Flat,* another stylized story, but one that has a certain restful and calming effect, with repeated adventures, all more or less the same, like in *Don Quixote.* And I thought some more about books that come to be read by posterity and those that are absorbed into the tastes and culture so that they don't need to be read. Which are the books that are perennially re-read? Those in which the essential thing is "form" —

certain poets, for example (Dante, Shakespeare, Goethe), who have given perfectly sculpted expression to certain attitudes and states of mind. You always come back to them when you want the thrill of that rich content enclosed in those few perfect verses. This is why great art is very often in the form of proverbs (and a "quotation" is not a form of proverb). Or you re-read the authors who, despite everything, failed to be assimilated by our tastes. Why do we re-read Plato? Basically, because he is distant and different from us. If he were a nearby relative we wouldn't need to read him. (You answer: then I must be very close to Plato, because I feel no need to read him). At this answer I am seized by an access of rage. I fling everything aside, tear up the letter, decide never to speak to you again of these serious and refined things, which you are unable to understand. I get upset, I torment myself, and I finish by declaring myself your most devoted and affectionate husband.

Your Eugenio

Being Victim of a Joke on April Fool's Day

Ventotene, April 2, 1941

My dear Ursel,

Yesterday I was the victim of an atrocious April fool's joke. Had I written that I had ordered some Angora rabbits? Well, Rossi and Spinelli, who had volunteered to get them for me, and after keeping me waiting for two months, had two paper-mache bunnies delivered to me yesterday, along with a nice fish. And to top it off they wanted me to pay for the drinks, which I energetically refused to do. So my beautiful rabbits, that I had gotten so excited about, are no more — but maybe it's better this way, because they would be very difficult to raise. Now we have an authentic brooding hen that hatches eggs like a fanatic, and tomorrow we're putting 15 eggs under her. We shall see.

Eugenio

Reading Hemingway

Ventotene, May 21, 1941

My dear wife,

I work a fair amount, and I read novels and books of philosophy, for example Jaspers on the philosophy of existence, which has nothing new to say and convinces me that these existentialist philosophers are toying with a problem that doesn't make sense. I'm reading the novel by Hemingway, the American writer. The argument is insipid, but beautifully described — young Americans who go from bar to bar, continually getting drunk. What I like about the description is its utter dryness, the absence of any sort of sentimental puffery. There is a boy who is jealous of a girl. You realize this from a dialogue in which he is in a bad mood and answers the girl with nothing but yes, no. When you come I'll read you a couple of pages and you'll see from that what I'm talking about. This evening I have half a mind to get *Zauberberg* by Thomas Mann. Can I do it? I'll let you know. I'd like also to read Bacchelli's trilogy, *The Mill on the Po*, which everyone talks about as a great novel. Maybe you could read it too. I write you these things because I imagine that in my absence your mood is intellectual. But I'm still convinced that intellectuality is not necessary at all. The things that are important are solving the problem of electromagnetism, having beautiful fat children, and above all loving my wife.

Your Eugenio

Living with the 'Soul' of a Writer, Not Becoming One

Ventotene, June 11, 1941

Ursel my dearest,

Even novels don't do much for me — I read the first volume of Bacchelli and flipped through the second, which I decided I won't read; I've started the umpteenth Huxley, but he is starting to make me sick with his snobbery and always satirizing the same types. In *Zauberberg* I am just now at the start of those fifty pages where he describes his grandfather, the senator, with the long hands and the collar where he hides his chin — a figure I know by heart from the 2000 pages of *Buddenbrooks*. I have a strong desire to skip them altogether, but I feel it would be dishonest to you; on the other hand

I'm afraid that if I take the time to read them, I'll end up not reading the book any more.

What writer is honest and direct, and writes with openness, sincerity and immediacy, not worried about "creating" anything, but writing only when there is something to say?

I had thought it was Huxley, but I'm afraid I was wrong. I think the fault is in the fact that for these people writing is a profession. If they didn't make money from their books, even the great writers would write only what they had to write. Therefore, my formula for the moment would be — live your life with the "soul" of a writer, but don't become one. I leave this to you in case it should be useful.

I embrace you, my only friend

Your Eugenio

Love as Unstable Equilibrium

Melfi, March 1, 1942

My dear,

I got your two letters of Sunday-Tuesday, as well as Wednesday's. The only thing I want to say is that at the moment what you write is the only thing I'm able to understand, and that it gives me great joy to read it. If there's one single thing you don't have to worry about it's writing in this tone, and that I might not understand. I don't think I have ever understood as well as I do now. I cannot answer you, and I don't want to; I just want to listen and for you to know that you can always speak.

Like you, I've been thinking a lot of things these days. For example that love is always a condition of unstable equilibrium and we're in trouble if it stops being that and turns into a stable one. And that just because it is an unstable equilibrium it is subject to sudden failure. But also that for this same reason the worst thing is to continually worry about keeping it, preserving it, protecting it. This is what turns it into a stable equilibrium, which means killing it. And so? So the only thing is to have the courage to face the unstable equilibrium, to be ready for anything, never sure about tomorrow. And to calmly imagine that perhaps tomorrow everything might be over.

Your Eugenio

The Discovery of the Possible

Being Idle and Natural

Melfi, March 3, 1942

Ursel,

You say to write about myself, but there's not much to tell. I do nothing all day, I stroll around, I chat, I amuse myself by taking on various attitudes, and sometimes by seeing how people talk among themselves. I like being seen as nice and that people seek out my company — in short, I behave a bit like a demagogue, but with one reservation — I have as little as possible to do with the set of brilliant ideas and insights I've stored up, which I no longer like and which in fact repel me. And then every so often I feel very different from the way I appear, and I get an intense urge to present myself as I really am — an urge that I repress out of modesty, and also because I see it as a sign of weakness and self-love. That said, I do not believe at all that this is a pose — on the contrary, it feels utterly natural to me. I have realized that it's much more human and natural to behave with various people according to what these various people mean to you. And that wanting to be yourself with everybody is a sign of profound egotism, or rather of weak and feminine love for yourself. Basically, I'm fairly happy, except for a certain nostalgia for my work, and a certain regret that I don't love it as madly as I once did. And I've realized that I'm not so old as I thought I was when I got here.

A hug from
Your Eugenio

Will to Live and Feeling Changed

Melfi, March 21, 1942

My friend,

I've just got your telegram that you won't come until next week. I hope the kids don't have anything serious. I was hoping you would come today, with the first day of spring. And I believe that says it all about my feelings as I wait for you. I don't know how our meeting will be. I read your letters from last week, and I can't answer because a week has already gone by, and I think that for you a week means a lot, as it does for me. I don't want anything except to live. I'm afraid I've achieved the position of a man who has freed himself of almost all his complexes, and there's nothing left for him but to live. Even work, ambition, the goals you set for yourself, seem like complexes, states of tension I can no longer identify with. And I'm afraid of this state, because in a certain way the emptiness of it bores me, its lack of purpose; but still I like it, it's very relaxing. I'm afraid you will find a very strange Eugenio Colorni of Trieste. Get ready to be disappointed. But then again, maybe not. You won't be able to say whether you like me, because I think your arrival will change a lot of things about me; although I can't imagine in what way. Come when you like, as you like; but don't feel you have to. And we'll tell each other whatever we like, and the only words we say will be the right ones. Why do I feel so sure and so unafraid? I don't think a man ever stops becoming a man, and it's a lot of fun.

Your Eugenio

Reading Rilke

Melfi, April 25, 1942

My dear,

"Time is not measured here; no year matters, and ten years are nothing. Being an artist means not reckoning and counting, but ripening like the tree which does not force its sap and stands confident in the storms of spring without the fear that the summer may not follow. It will. But it comes only to the patient, who stand there as though eternity lay before them, so untroubled, still and open. I learn it daily, learn it in pain to which I am grateful: patience is everything!"

I've transcribed these lines because I read them for you and they belong to a book you love [Rainer Maria Rilke's *Letters to a Young Poet*]; not because they have any particular application to you or me. But they are beautiful and right, consoling and noble. Joy for a spirit that has achieved a certain richness, and can let itself live! . . . And if the work of art arrives, good; if not, that's good as well. The same book says that "A work of art is valuable when it is born of necessity." Lucky the man for whom this motto is not a stern call for parsimony and control, but rather a consolation for laziness, the promise of a gift that one day will arrive without being too keenly desired.

Your Eugenio

Rilke: Spiritual Creation and Physical Delight

Melfi, April 27, 1942

"... for spiritual creation also springs from the physical, is of one nature with it, only like a gentler, more ecstatic and more everlasting repetition of physical delight.... In one creative thought a thousand forgotten nights of love revive, filling it with majesty and exaltation."

I cannot help but go on transcribing passages for you from the same book, which I'm reading the way an 18-year-old girl would read it — looking for passages that relate to me and marking them with love and passion. It is a perfect little thing, to be held close like a beautiful jewel or picture.

Eugenio

Rilke: Love Is Difficult

Melfi, May 2, 1942

"Auch lieben ist gut: denn Liebe ist schwer. Liebhaben von Mensch zu Mensch: das ist vielleicht das schwerste, was uns aufgegeben ist, das Äusserste, die letzte Probe und Prüfung, die Arbeit, für die alle andere Arbeit nur Vorbereitung ist."[17]

It's just perfect! Right, true — such words don't do it justice.
A big hug.
Eugenio

Rilke: Love Helps You Becoming a World

Melfi, May 3, 1942

That bit I transcribed for you yesterday goes on in a way that I only partly like. It says that love "ist ein erhabener Anlass für den Einzelnen, zu reifen, in sich etwas zu werden, Welt zu werden, Welt zu werden für sich um eines anderen Willen, es ist ein grosser Anspruch an ihn, etwas, was ihn auserwählt und zu Weitem beruft. Nur in diesem Sinne, als Aufgabe an sich zu arbeiten («zu horchen und zu hämmern Tag und Nacht») dürften junge Menschen die Li-

---

[17] "To love is good, too, because love is difficult. For one human being to love another — that is perhaps the most difficult of all our tasks, the ultimate, the last test and proof, the work for which all other work is but preparation."

ebe, die ihnen gegeben wird, gebrauchen."[18]

No doubt this is true — actually it is true, but I don't like him saying it. It is true that love makes you mature and helps you become a "world." But taking love as an opportunity, a tool for growing up, this is exactly what keeps you from growing up. In love the towering figure is the other, not you; and so the hell with *Einsamkeit* [loneliness]. I want to be loved by you more than anything, but not because I need to be loved; rather because I wish I could give you love's joy and pain, its brimming heart, soul and senses, its *Hilflosigkeit* [helplessness]. I wish I had given it to you so that it was yours and could help you grow and flourish.

Your Eugenio

Your Ability as a Young Woman Understanding Rilke

Melfi, May 9, 1942

Dear,

I've been thinking about your last two letters. It seems strange to me that at 16–19 you were able to identify with a book like Rilke's letters. My impression is that I've had to toil my way through 33 years to understand it. If I had read it at 18, the things he says would have struck me as completely uninteresting. I would have thought, "Yes, beautiful, well said, but he would have been equally justified saying exactly the opposite." I would never have seen why they are beautiful just the way they are. That you should have understood this at that age seems monstrous; or, more simply, it's the great superiority women have (real women, how few there are!) at being receptive by instinct, and not, like us, by laborious conquest.

Eugenio

---

[18] "It is a high inducement to the individual to mature, to become something in himself, to become a world, to become a world for himself and for another's sake, it is a great exacting claim upon him, something that seeks him out and calls him to vast things. Only in this sense, as the task of working on themselves ("to hearken and to hammer day and night"), can young people use the love that is given them."

Down with Style in Literature

Melfi, May 17, 1942

Dearest,

I'm just finishing *Thunder on the Left*, which is a pretty little thing and creates an atmosphere quite effectively. But it is not a masterpiece, which from its tone it evidently would like to be. I think fifty years from now when people read sentences like this: "The single swathe of sunshine carved the hall, dividing it into two dusks as the word now divides one's mind," it will have the same effect as the "agudezas" [witticisms] of the high Baroque have today. It's pointless — the only art that can claim to last has to be immediate, honest, direct, not "contrived," not "showing off," not stylized. Every style, every taste, by its nature is bound to by "entlarvt" [unmasked] and to disappear. Down with style. The sign of mature art, in my view, is precisely that it does not need the crutch of style. Look at Stendhal, Goethe, Nietzsche. And then look, by contrast, at Th. Mann, Proust, Kafka.

Warm hugs,
Your Eugenio

My Affinity with Reichenbach

Melfi, May 18, 1942

Dear,

I'm now thoroughly launched into my work, once again with the old stamina, which shows itself in my irritation when someone comes looking for me, etc. Reichenbach's is the first book I've found, after 5 years of research, that contains my idea. And note that I've never found this book mentioned, while many books by the same author are cited frequently. This shows that if I had published my ideas just as they were, they would have had no effect. Naturally this has no influence at all on my work, which sets its sights much further down the road; but it will serve as a useful check. And I suspect there are some errors in it (which is possible in this case, since it is an "isolated" book that is not at all part of the body of received doctrine).

Warm hugs,
Eugenio

Part III

1. Ursula Hirschmann: "A Letter of Eugenio's: Melfi 1942"[19]

Putting some old papers in order, I came across a copy of a letter from Eugenio Colorni to the *Podestà*[20] of Melfi. The letter is dated 28 June 1942. Living with me and our young daughters, Colorni was at the time a political internee at Melfi. The letter, written by hand on a sheet of foolscap, reads as follows:

"To the Podestà of the Municipality of Melfi,
I the undersigned Eugenio Colorni, political internee in the Municipality of Melfi, have read Your Lordship's order, Protocol n. 8461, which obliges me to display the national flag today, throughout the course of the day, from the window of my dwelling.

Considering that because of my condition as a political internee I have been expressly forbidden to conduct any sort of manifestation of a political nature, or to participate in any type of public ceremony, I find that I am unable to comply with the order received.

Since Your Lordship believes that the failure to display the national flag at the window of my house may disturb the public order, I will in no way — as I stated previously — oppose the flag's being displayed by appointees of the Podestà who have been expressly delegated for the purpose.

In perfect compliance,
Eugenio Colorni
Melfi, 28 June 1942."

The letter was sent by hand to the town hall and that same evening my husband was arrested and a report was made to the magistrate. He remained in prison for a day or two, and was released on parole pending a ruling from the judge.

By chance, the judge lived in a small house next to ours on the

---
[19] *la Repubblica,* 12 October 1986.
[20] Head of the municipal administration during the fascist era.

recently widened and asphalted road leading from the distant railway station through small gardens and modest villas up the hill on which the old city rose. Every morning we saw the magistrate leave his house and make his way to his office in an ancient building up in the city. He was a small, thin man, pale and decrepit. We exchanged greetings when we met.

His wife remained at home. She was a plump young woman with thick, loose hair, whom I heard singing while she did the housework; when I went out with the girls she had usually finished what there was to do and was there at the window, leaning on a velvet cushion. The girls greeted her gaily, and once I motioned to her from my side window to come over and visit us. She smiled and answered me with a gesture of helplessness.

At Ventotene, where we had been previously, I had got used to the fact that the respectable people there did not mix with the internees, because it would have cast them in a bad light with the authorities, and I thought this must also be the case for the magistrate's wife. At Melfi, however, this rule was not generally observed, and I mentioned the thing one day to the corner tobacconist with whom I was friendly. She glanced at her daughter and laughed, and explained to me that there was another reason the judge's wife could not come see me — the little magistrate shut her in the house every morning, out of jealousy; obviously she had got used to this, singing every morning as she did the housework. Then in the afternoon she put away her apron and, beautifully turned out, strolled into town arm in arm with her husband, and came back with her bag filled with shopping.

This was the magistrate who now would judge my husband. The outlook wasn't bright. Imagine a man who shut his wife in the house, a little man in a worn out dark suit with shiny elbows, setting himself against "His Lordship the Podestà," the rich and flashy son of landowners, who swanned around in the company of the *Federale* [Fascist Party Secretary], both looking disdainful in their neatly-cut uniforms and with an obvious desire to teach a lesson to this Milanese professor with the foreign wife who wrote punctilious letters that almost seemed to make fun of them!

The magistrate no longer greeted us and we avoided him so as not to embarrass him. Only our daughters kept on obliviously calling to the lady at the window. . . .

The day of judgment arrived, and after the initial formalities it was over in a matter of minutes. The little magistrate, perhaps even more pale than usual, but with a voice that was firm and a bit strident, explained that professor Eugenio Colorni had been sent into political internment by the tribunal because he was antifascist, that he could not now be blamed for something he had already been convicted of, that being antifascist he could not be expected to want to display the fascist flag, and that therefore he was acquitted effective immediately. The proceedings were closed.

Once again there was something to be learned here. Private backwardness doesn't always mean falling into line with power. The civic courage of this man was in its way superior to ours. Because of course we had our ideas in opposition to the regime, but so did our friends — indeed, our whole "environment." While he, in that hall, seemed entirely alone, his responsibility as a judge lifting him above the political climate in which he lived. We thought that as long as a country had judges like him in Melfi and other places there was room for hope that the fascist regime would not last forever.

2. Last Wishes of Eugenio Colorni[21]

These are the last wishes of Eugenio Colorni, son of Alberto, born in Milan on 22 April 1909.

I appoint as my universal heir for all intents and purposes (naturally excepting the part due by law to my daughters, and the legacies indicated below) my wife Ursula Hirschmann, to whom I entrust the education of our three daughters Silvia, Renata, Eva, confirming my full confidence in her. For my little ones, who will be without a father or brothers, I refrain from offering any counsel or advice — their mother's sure intuition will guide them in life, and at the same time, public morals and customs will undergo such a radical upheaval in the coming years that I cannot offer any guidelines regarding their education. I would just urge them to consider love as the most serious and important thing in life; the thing that brings us close to another being so that we forget ourselves and want that person to live in their own essence, so very different from ours. I would urge them not to squander their feelings, not to mistake superficial and passing excitement for love. These same wishes go to my wife, whom I bless along with our three little ones, hoping with all my heart that she finds the serene happiness that my incapable, unhappy, desperate love was never able to give her.

I advise my wife to seek help and support in administering the inheritance from my brother-in-law, Willi Schwarz, whom I designate executor of my will.

To my sister Silvia I would like to leave an important object that may remind her often of her brother — but I don't remember anything of mine that suits the purpose. She herself, in agreement with my wife, will know the right thing to choose.

To my brother-in-law Willi Schwarz I leave the Longines watch that belonged to my father, with its chain.

---

[21]Testament written by Eugenio Colorni on May 2, 1943, published in AA.VV. (2011a), 283–84.

To my brother-in-law Otto Albert Hirschmann, in whom I seemed to have found a younger brother, I leave all the personal possessions that my wife and daughters don't need. I entrust my wife with the task of looking among my things for some objects to be given as keepsakes to my mother-in-law Hedwig Hirschmann, my sister-in-law Eva Hirschmann, and my three nieces Laura, Clara and Susanna Schwarz.

To my mother-in-law Hedwig Hirschmann I leave the sum of L. 100,000 (one hundred thousand). Only, however, in the case that my whole estate is valued at more than one million lire. I entrust this assessment to Willi Schwarz.

Any books that my wife does not need should be distributed among my friends: Altiero Spinelli, Otto Albert Hirschmann, Guido Morpurgo Tagliabue, Ernesto Rossi, Ludovico Geymonat, Willi Schwarz. I entrust this distribution to Guido Morpurgo Tagliabue. I leave my manuscripts and scientific typescripts to Ludovico Geymonat. If he has the will and patience to use my puerile and incomplete notes to trace the main line of my research, and either make use of it as his own or transmit it to others, one of my most vivid desires will have been fulfilled.

The same goes for my philosophical and literary manuscripts, which I entrust to Guido Morpurgo Tagliabue. I don't care about being cited or publicly remembered. The only thing dear to me is the thought that I will continue for a while to be a part of my friends' conversations — those conversations which were perhaps the purest joy of my life.

If it isn't too much trouble, I would like to be buried in Milan, in the tomb of my parents; or possibly cremated.

Faithfully,
Eugenio Colorni

3. LETTER TO ALTIERO SPINELLI[22]

Pantagruelian Attitude, Political 'Ideology,' and a Future Action for the European Unity[23]

May 1943

I

{Dear Altiero,
You may not like the letter I am about to write; it is meant to be, if *not* an indictment, at least an attempt to clarify the reasons for the dissatisfaction aroused in many of us by your actions over the last two years. It is a dissatisfaction you feel yourself, if I do *not* misread your acts of impatience, intolerance, and irritation, which strike me as those of someone who feels in a vague way that he has not entirely got into gear. In my opinion, the reasons for this inadequacy lie in two psychological attitudes that I will try briefly to clarify before putting things in more purely political terms.

1) Your "Pantagruelian" attitude, which you defined in your "dialogue on detachment"[24] and your "autobiography."[25] It's an attitude for which I have great admiration and sympathy (I expressed this,

---

[22]Letter published in Spinelli, A. (1993), 190–203.
[23]The letter exists in the Spinelli Fund in two typed drafts that differ from each other in some parts. The first, indicated here as "A," is longer than the second, indicated "B." since it contains an introduction that is not present in the second copy. Copy A has no indications, while B has a handwritten note at the top, "Ready for printing." The title of copy B is "The Practical Implementation of European Unity. A Discussion Among Federalists," successively crossed out and replaced with "What Forces Are Operating Today in the Direction of European Unity?" Included here are the complete text of copy "B" plus the additions taken from the copy "A" put between curly brackets { }. Only copy A is signed [note by Piero Graglia]. In all likelihood, copy "B," along with Spinelli's answer and that of Colorni published below (Eugenio Colorni to Altiero Spinelli) were meant to compose a mimeographed booklet, which never appeared.
[24]Cf. Eurostudium3w, July-September 2007.
[25]Cf. "Nota autobiografica per Rossi dopo le maldicenze fatte presso di lui da varia gente" [Autobiographical note for Rossi after he was slandered by various people], in Spinelli A. (1993).

in fact, in a "dialogue on death," which I never sent you[26]). It is one of the most exalted and generous of human attitudes. It is not at all, however, the attitude of a modern politician, of someone, that is, who wants to achieve certain goals. It is the attitude of the entertainer, the teacher, the person who exudes warmth, who only needs to appear and people will follow him. Undoubtedly, some politicians have been of this type. But will tomorrow's political struggles really present themselves in these terms? Will the masses in search of direction really turn toward this kind of political attitude?

You accepted this as an unproven dogma, as an implicit premise. You started out assuming that at the end of the war the floodgates are suddenly going to open and the waters will rush down and submerge everything. And you assigned to yourself and whoever follows you the task of digging the great channel that will guide these waters and make them once again beneficial and fertile. In effect, this is what happened in many European countries in 1918. Will it happen again this time? It's a problem I will address on its own later. I don't believe the possibility has ever occurred to you that things might not go this way. Because of a certain mental inertia that always makes us picture things in a way that will favor the fulfillment of our own prospects, you keep imagining situations in which the unleashed and disoriented masses are looking for a guide, a beacon that will light their way. And you correctly propose that you will be such a guide for them — with greater intelligence and impartiality, with greater attention and attachment to the concrete situation and the needs of the moment than the traditional parties are capable of.

But what if things don't go this way? What if tomorrow's postwar period doesn't present this fluid and chaotic aspect, this new primordial state where victory is there to be seized by whoever has the most open mind and the stoutest heart?

It's a hypothesis you've never even considered, it seems so absurd. Or you've considered it only to discard it immediately, rejecting the idea that the old traditional parties have the strength to channel the floodwaters into their old and worn-out furrows. But have you ever wondered if there might not be new forces much more power-

---

[26]Now in Colorni, E. (2009).

ful than the old parties, which are already irretrievably directing the waters into channels that are indeed well-defined? We'll talk about this later. But it is precisely your inability (which is obvious to everyone) to face this possibility; it is precisely your horror at a situation that is not "Pantagruelian" — it is precisely this that sometimes makes your words sound empty and tired. You have planted yourself in the middle of the current, you've built your embankment, and now you're surprised that so little water is swirling past it. You get irritated, exasperated: 'Quit your fussing, roll up your sleeves and get to work.' But the fact is that there where you have planted yourself there is hardly any water. The waters are rapidly opening channels further down, along other banks that carry them more or less in the same direction as yours. But you don't notice. Those banks are not yours. They're made of a kind of cement that you don't trust. So you prefer not to consider them; not to see them.

I wouldn't want you to confuse these accusations of mine with the accusation, so often made against you, of having a "dictatorial spirit." It's not this that I'm criticizing you for. It is rather this "fever for action," which leads you to imagine that you are always in a central position, when in fact your position is peripheral. It's not that your 'Pantagruelian' way is disagreeable or unbearable, or that it offends my sense of freedom and independence. On the contrary, I like it very much and it doesn't offend me at all. But it makes you fall into errors of perspective and make blunders — that's all.

2) The second thing I want to reproach you for is not so much a personal defect as having let yourself be dragged into a sin that is very common among those forced to practice politics in prison, confinement or exile. It is what I would call the sin of "ideology." I have recently had occasion to observe this first hand in people who had made politics the only reason for their existence. They had the same defects and shortcomings that we have so often criticized and laughed at in philosophers. They too built themselves beautiful palaces where they put everything they required, all their "needs," all their "ideals of civilization." For them too, the main worry was whether the palace would stand up in its logical coherence, in its "circularity." A political ideology and a philosophical system are in

this sense like two peas in a pod. The aim in one case is to reconcile in dialectic harmony being and becoming, freedom and necessity, the finite and the infinite; and in the other freedom and authority, socialism and democracy, etc. You yourself have noted with a certain irony that for some time our politicians have been trying to find the right dosages of these things; but you too, perhaps drawn in by your arguments with them, have in the end not been doing anything different. You too are looking for the formula that will overcome Marxism. You too want to give the word socialism its most correct and modern definition; you too are preparing your socialist sauce seasoned with liberalism to enter in the competition with the others. Not that these things aren't important, but right now they strike me as a bit abstract. And just as philosophy does not make progress by resolving eternal problems, but rather by rigorously meditating on particular facts, procedures and methods, and leaving the general systemic position in the background, deliberately inaccurate and only hinted at; so also politics, in my view, will not move forward by retouching its ideological structure, setting out the formulations and solutions for eternal problems; but by keeping its eye on developing events and trying to influence them using the most effective and unbiased methods; always, of course, in the light of some basic positions which it should be enough to have clear in one's heart and, I would say, in one's instincts, without needing to bend all your efforts toward giving them a clear and exact and logical formulation.

At this point I can hear you sigh with irritation at my eternal psychologizing, and appeal to me to talk about concrete problems and not states of mind. And that is exactly what I'm about to do. This preamble was not intended as anything more than the premise for a series of political observations}.

Dear Altiero, I would like to clarify some points of disagreement between us concerning the position to be adopted regarding the events that may occur in the near future. Many things have changed since our discussions of two years ago. I will enumerate for you some things that over the last two years I don't think you have given sufficient consideration to {you have noticed}.

{3) I said in part 1 that} The implicit premise of your whole political edifice is that at the end of this war the masses will run wild in movements that are violent and disorderly; and that the political victory will go to whoever can gain their favor and direct the force of these movements toward a clear and determined end. You stand out from the other parties in your desire to review and update the old ideologies and your lack of trust in old battle lines and slogans. But what you have in common with them is your method of fighting, which consists of going before the people, getting them to follow you, and throwing the weight of this approval into the political struggle. In this sense you maintain (always implicitly) that nothing has changed since 1918. You imagine that now, as then, the postwar period will be marked by enormous fluctuations in popular favor, following this or that man, this or that ideology.

Is it now paradoxical to think that this is not the way things will go? It is so only for those who want to see nothing more in the situation than their own desires and habitual ways of thinking.

The victorious nations of the last war tried to dominate the defeated states through territorial mutilation, military restrictions, economic and financial burdens. But they were not remotely concerned with influencing domestic politics. Germany, Austria, Turkey, Greece, and Italy were left in the grip of their own internal upheavals, "free," as it was put at the time, "to choose the regime they thought suitable." The only attempt to intervene was in Russian politics, and this was utterly without success. The principle of "non intervention" was part of inter-war political morals, and it was the fascists first and then the communists who set it aside in the Spanish war.

Now I don't know how the winners will treat the losers at the end of this war. But one thing I do know for sure — this time they will not make the mistake of staying out of domestic politics. Intentions are very clear on this point; and not a day goes by when they are not reaffirmed by all parties involved. They want to destroy the fascist regimes once and for all, and no resurgence of nationalisms, chauvinisms, etc. will be countenanced. The distinctively ideological character of this war is what guarantees that the victorious states will not leave the losers to their own devices. And this will also be the weapon they use to fight against each other, each trying to gain influence over the other and cement its own predominance in Europe.

Each of the two winners has a special apparatus for this purpose, and to achieve their aims they are ready to implement the powerful tools of propaganda, police, and espionage, along with economic and military intimidation.

As a result, the political life of all the peoples of Europe will be dominated by this factor, which will decisively influence mass movements and give them a very special character that they did not have at the end of the other war. This time we are in the presence of two very powerful state organizations that present themselves as paladins of the two basic ideologies contending for the European field. Fighting for one of these ideologies will mean, not only implicitly but in the general consciousness of the people, fighting in favour of the corresponding power. The communism-democracy antithesis has gradually transformed itself into a Russia-England antithesis.

Is this good or bad? We will find out later. But it is a fact that would be foolish to ignore, and it will establish the ironclad initial conditions for the fluid and chaotic state which, as I have said, our mental inertia tends to represent to us as the immediate postwar situation. Once the great dikes have burst, the surging waters will not be free to flow in just any direction; they will be irresistably drawn into the two huge conduits that are being readied to receive them. It will be in our power to help deviate them from one to the other. But wanting to oppose this, or to act as if it didn't exist, wanting to persist in presenting yourself to the people in the old way in hopes of rousing them through the clarity and honesty of your vision and the courage and resolution of your actions — this may be desirable and agreeable; but it's as if you were fighting alongside Garibaldi, rushing headlong and bare-chested at the enemy in an age of machine guns and tanks.

It is a historical phenomenon of tremendous import, representing perhaps the most essential difference between the 1918 situation and that of today. At that time the different ideologies, the different ways humanity wanted to configure its own existence, found their natural expression in political parties. Today they look to something stronger for support — the immense military, economic, political and organizational power of nations. Today there are three states (Russia, Germany, England) that represent in a nutshell the three basic types of political life known to our civilization. All three claim the right to organize Europe as they see fit. This war will eliminate one of them from the contest. The other two remain — and it is very likely that the struggle between them will not be fought — at least at first — with weapons, but rather with foreign policy, and even more at the level of domestic politics — each trying to attract to itself the various countries of Europe, maneuvering and influencing the various political currents in them, creating blocs and counter-blocs. And the various political parties will be nothing more than pawns in this immense game. Like it or not, it is in this sort of situation that we will find we have to operate.

2) {4} – Like it or not. The first reaction of people who think of a return to the situation of 1918 is not to like it. So they try involuntarily not to notice it. And if they do take account of it, they disapprove; they oppose it with all their might. "We want to be masters of our own destiny," they say. "We don't want to be anyone's protégés; we don't want to go along; we don't want to be the Quislings in this situation. If Europe is to be created, it will be by the will of Europeans, not by the ambition of this or that victorious nation."

Let us look at how things actually are. One of the most serious difficulties that arose when we began to conceive of European unity as the central postwar problem was to educate the masses and political parties to think and operate in international terms, rather than within the narrow limits of local and national problems. A European rallying cry — it was said — could have little grip on public consciousness, except during the very brief period of demobilization. As soon as political life returns more or less to normal, the masses will turn to the problems closest to their immediate interests; a prolonged education will be needed to accustom them to a broader and more comprehensive view of things. It was precisely this contrast between the urgency of the European problem and the public's unpreparedness to solve it that was the main problem for our program and the reason it was accused by others of being utopian. It seemed that a rallying cry that was international would necessarily fall on deaf ears with the public.

And now we are actually in the presence of an international rallying cry, imposed by virtue of its own strength, which presents itself to the masses as the only solution that is concrete and real and responds to the actual situation. We see it before us and we don't recognize it for what it is — are we going to reject it then because it is damaging to our autonomy and our freedom of action? We see that events themselves are taking shape more or less as we would have wished — do we nevertheless refuse to recognize this, only because it isn't happening in the form and style that we had initially hoped for? Only because things have worked out so that the forces we were counting on have so far had no role to play?

This rallying cry, whose power the masses today find irresistible — clearer, simpler, more elementary than any social or political ideology — is this: Russia or England. It is into these terms that the public translates, with confident instinct, every political speech they hear. I do not want to deny that this can arouse a certain melancholy. It betrays the widespread sense in the masses that the initiative has slipped out of their hands, that there are now more powerful forces deciding their destinies; it betrays their awareness that political ideologies have now become embodied in a well-defined state apparatus and have lost the liveliness and immediacy they once had. It expresses that sense of the passivity of the popular forces that has been so often evident during this war; that vague awareness of being tools in the hands of forces superior to them; only easy and thoughtless enthusiasm can lead one to imagine this disappearing at a stroke at the end of the war.

And yet, having said all this, the slogan is in fact typically "European." It is seen as common sense by all the peoples of Europe. It expresses an awareness that postwar problems will be solved at an international level; it identifies two powerful centers of unification for our continent. Trying to deny that the presence of this slogan in the consciousness of the masses represents a huge step forward on the road to European unity means not seeing beyond your own nose. This step forward happened in a very different way from what we had imagined. Our sort of upbringing and culture had no part in it. But if we have indeed decided, and not as a joke, to put the problem of European unity at the center of our efforts, we will have to acknowledge this reality as it exists, and base ourselves on it as a positive element pointing the way we have to march. Thinking in a

European sense means first of all moving the center of one's vision.

Europe today is not an undifferentiated mass such that a unifying center could be indiscriminately created just anywhere. These centers exist in well-defined places, visible to all. We need their backing if we do not want to fall once again into nationalistic particularism or empty utopianism. In the Europe of today, Italy has a strange, peripheral position, which can nevertheless be decisive for unification. Anyone who wants to take action in Italy must accept this position, and cannot behave as if we were at the center, the starting point of the movement, or as if the center could be anywhere. "But in that case," you say, "what should we do? Wait for others to take the initiative and then politely support it? Try to more or less subtly influence the ruling classes of the winning states, so that they happily accept their role as the initiators of a European unity that favors their interests?"

I would now like to show you that this is not what we're talking about.

3) {5} – There is yet another thing I'm afraid you are not sufficiently aware of. Two years ago, when we were thinking about the unity of Europe, it presented itself as a goal to be reached in a single leap, in the period immediately after the cessation of hostilities. "It is essential," we said, "that we not wait for the hot lava to re-solidify in the old molds. We need to strike while the iron is hot, and see to it that when the victors sit down at the peace conference table to give Europe a new orientation, they find before them a Europe already launched on the road to unification by the revolutionary strength of its people. If we can't seize this chance at the opportune moment, we will have lost it forever; and the unification of Europe will have to be put off until the end of the Third World War."

This is more or less what we were thinking two years ago. Have the prospects changed in these two years? I would say they have. It's clear by now that at the end of this war Europe will find itself split into two areas of influence that are profoundly different in terms of political orientation as well as cultural and economic structure. What the line of demarcation will be, whether there will be buffer states between them, etc., we cannot at the moment foresee. Nor can we predict how the two winners will exert their influence on the states under their domination — whether by actual annexation (especially Russia) or by exercising political, economic and military control. In any case, it's clear by now that once the two areas of influence have been established, the whole postwar period will be dominated by an open or covert struggle between the victorious powers, by the attempted expansion of one at the expense of the other, and by their efforts to take control of key positions. The site of this struggle will be the continent of Europe, and it is clear that the people of Europe will not remain passive. On the contrary, the character of the contest will depend to a great extent on them — whether it will burn itself out in a simple imperialist clash between Russia and England, or whether it will be the starting point for the effective unification of the continent. One way or the other, what emerges from this perspective is that the struggle for European unity will no longer be limited to the narrow time frame between the end of hostilities and the conclusion of the peace, but will have at its disposal the broader postwar period. The last two years, I believe, have brought about this change in our prospects and made them vastly more concrete and feasible than they were before. Even here, events are moving the way we wanted, with or without us. It is a question of noticing this and taking it into account.

The two winning states, each the arbiter of a piece of our continent, have two paths open to them. One is a policy of housekeeping, of internal reconstruction, reinforcing the ruling class, repaying their own people for their sacrifices during the war by improving their economic conditions and promoting their psychological position as 'winners'; keeping the countries in their own sphere of influence in a state of economic and military semi-subjugation, covertly sabotaging any real revolutionary effort they might make, any attempt to clean house to make way for renewal. Or, there is the other path — joining with the vanquished, constituting with them a true and deeply-rooted unity; absorbing their lifeblood and civilizing forces; reconstructing together, sharing power with their ruling classes and letting them participate in leading the new unity being created; and facing the other half of Europe as a compact, aggressive bloc, endowed with an immensely strong power of popular attraction.

The two winners will oscillate continually between these two extremes. From a purely nationalistic point of view, the first option would represent a reinforcement of nationalist structures and would safeguard them against yesterday's enemies; but the second would allow very active and independent policy choices vis-a-vis the other winner, which would be prevented from extending its tentacles into the first winner's sphere of influence to try to break it up and win it over.

Even imperialist aims, broadly intended, might be advanced for either of the two victorious powers by a European policy. But certainly a decisive element in determining the choice is the concrete situation that is created in the countries within their spheres of influence. We can be sure, for example, that whatever desire for peace and domestic tranquillity there may be in Russian leadership circles, they cannot remain disinterested if a widespread revolutionary movement should break out — as it quite likely will — in nearby Germany. If the Germans are determined enough to take charge of their own destiny and impose on their own people this revolution they have long been ready for, the Russians will not be able to resist intervening and favoring unification. This will of course initially be under their direction, but it will soon give rise to a mixed class of leadership with a distinctly European character. In short, *it is in the power of the peoples of Europe to force the winning powers to come out of their nationalistic shell and to set in motion, even in spite of themselves, a policy of European unification.* They will be able to create in Europe de facto states that the winners, in their own interests, cannot ignore. They can see to it that the situation breaks in one direction or the other.

This is the high card in their hands. A card that will need to be played in actions involving the masses; not based on abstract federalist ideology, but rather stressing something people will be more than ready for — the fact that it is their attitude, every time, that can decide the outcome of a particular development in international politics, moving it in one direction or the other. Is this the action of a Quisling? In pushing them to act in our interests are we a fifth column in the winners' camp? I don't think so. It is more like the action of the men of the Risorgimento, who organized uprisings and movements all over the peninsula for the purpose of provoking intervention and making sure the international situation would come down on the side of Italian Unity.

4) {6°} — From what I've said, you can deduce what I think of the "European Federalist Movement." While participating wholeheartedly in the pursuit of its avowed purpose, I charge it with the defect of building the model of the perfect European federation too carefully, forgetting to observe the many outcomes of the drastic moves made by the countless forces on today's political chessboard — outcomes which, sometimes following unexpected paths that we could hardly have imagined, have served our own purposes. Only if we have the openness to recognize these formidable forces, and to embed our activity in their framework, only then will we get out of the field of noble ideology and into that of concrete action.
{Eugenio}
May 1943

4. Letter to Altiero Spinelli[27]

Post-war Germany, Collectivism, and Market

Dear Altiero,[28]

Your letter has the virtue of clarifying the situation completely and leaves no room for misunderstanding. It is what I had tried to begin to do myself, and I'm glad you've continued it so honestly. Whatever conclusions we draw from our discussions, we will have reached them for good reasons and can be sure that we are not deceiving or deluding each other.

I am willing to accept almost all the observations you make in your analysis of the situation — I agree with you that "the revolution Germany has long been ready for" is nothing other than the communist revolution. I never meant to say otherwise. And your ongoing irony about the "inspired state of mind" of someone who sees this revolution as a "mystical event," etc. is lost on me, since I don't believe I have ever suffered from such a malady. I also accept what you say when you state that my judgment on the progressive or reactionary nature of Russia and England hinges on the support or hostility these countries offer the German revolution. It isn't sympathy or antipathy toward countries that motivates my judgment, but the ability I see in them to make up a bloc that might be the nucleus of a future united Europe.

I also agree with you that a communist revolution in Germany would strengthen "mass civilization" in that country at the expense of "individualist civilization"; and I have no illusions that "bringing about a collectivist transformation in Germany could completely change the German character."

And finally, I also agree that a Russo-German bloc set on the conquest of Europe would in all probability bring about a third

---

[27]Letter of June-July 1943 published in Spinelli, A. (1993), 213–18
[28]This letter follows the answer of Altiero Spinelli of May 1943 (now in Spinelli, A. 1993, 203–12. For the date of this letter, cf. 173.

world war (but, I hasten to add, it would truly be a definitive war for European unity, and not for European equilibrium like the two previous wars; it would be a war to achieve European unity now. In the Italian Risorgimento there were three wars. And I am not at all sure that to best implement and complete European unity a third war may not be necessary. Today the issue is to make sure that the present war constitutes a decisive step in that direction, and that we don't return to the status quo. That is, to make sure that any third war is not once again a war for European equilibrium).

As you see, our perspectives on the situation are more or less in agreement. It is concerning its solution that our viewpoints diverge. You insist on "individualist civilization"; I on European unity. You would reject a united Europe that was not based on "individualist civilization"; I would reject an individualist civilization that wasn't based on European unity. Just to avoid misunderstandings I will cite your words: "a Russo-German communist bloc would mean that the eastern border of Europe would return to roughly what was in Augustus's time... Beyond the border collectivist and militaristic countries, bent on conquering continents, on this side countries that under Anglo-American guidance would convulsively try to save something of European civilization." Faced with the prospect of a Russian-German unification of Europe, your concern then would be to block it for the purpose of saving something of European civilization. Mine would be to facilitate it and hurry it along in every way.

As you can see, this isn't about political logic, or working out a line of reasoning down to the final consequences; it's rather that the situation, having become clear to a certain degree, imposes a choice that each of us must make according to our own leanings and sympathies, our own cultural and moral needs — a choice, therefore, that is very difficult to discuss with a cool head. What is clear up to now in our discussion is the possibility (if not probability) that we will one day find ourselves having to take a position regarding the prospect of a communist Russo-German initiative for European unification. I would go further — it is possible that the position of our country and the attitude of its people are exactly what might cause one side or the other to collapse — that is, either hastening a process of unification based on successive annexations or favoring a stiffening of western Europe for the purpose of saving "individualist civilization" and setting off the Third World War. We may find ourselves, one day not far off, facing this sobering responsibility. Are you really sure the decision you've made is already irrevocable?

It is somewhat painful, for reasons given above, to lay out for you the motives that prompt me to accept the prospect of a European union based on "mass civilization." I have done so on other occasions, in discussions that were not among our best. Nevertheless I will try to set down some points.

1st — In your essay "Marxist and federalist politics,"[29] you stated clearly that a collectivist economy is the only one adapted to a country at war, or in the grip of serious difficulties that threaten its very existence. And you also argued that a "market" economy contains within it no guarantee of its own stability, apart from assuring the development of certain social groups interested in maintaining it (I don't have the essay with me to offer a precise citation, but I don't think I've mistaken your meaning). Now I believe that a unified or unifying Europe will be obliged for a fairly long period to consider itself in a state of war, or at least a state of emergency. The make or break issue for this union will be the establishment of a collectivist regime. And if I'm not mistaken, your own argument with the liberals, and your clash with them, resulted from your assertion that the construction of Europe would require an initial period that was authoritarian, dictatorial, and collectivist.[30] The people capable of seriously and coherently launching such a regime are, by your own admission, the communists.

---

[29]Colorni refers to one of the federalist essays written on the island immediately after the *Manifesto*. His reference to "your essay" in the plural, which would seem to indicate the participation of Rossi in the drafting of "Marxist and federalist politics," simply indicates the extent to which the views of Spinelli and Rossi coincided in this period; things that the two of them wrote individually were often attributed to both. At the same time the distinction helps Colorni differentiate his own position from that of the two authors of the *Manifesto*. Cf. the text of the essay in question, written between 1942 and 1943, in A. Spinelli (1985) [note by Piero Graglia].
[30]Cf. Spinelli, A. (1993), 115–23.

2nd — What makes you deprecate a communist solution, despite your approval of an initial dictatorship, is your position that for the communists, dictatorship and economic collectivism are ends in themselves; they are permanent methods of governance, not simply temporary expedients. Now I would argue that communism (especially a European variety) is much more capable of evolving than you think. I think it is unprejudiced in economic matters, and is thus far linked to a collectivist and autarchic economy in Russia only because of that country's frantic need to prepare for war. I think that even in the area of culture there would be a "Europa capta ferum victorem coepit,"[31] or at least that it would be our task — and a feasible one — to see that this happened. I am inclined to believe that the degree of "individualist civilization" in any regime does not depend so much on its institutional structure, its functionaries' goodwill or the ideologies that dominate it, as on the accumulation of difficulties and internal and external dangers that it finds it has to face. A regime in a state of war and in the grip of a serious economic crisis, or in a phase of unstable settlement can afford very little "individualism"; on the other hand "individualism" arises as a spontaneous bloom even in the most typically authoritarian and collectivist structures, once there is a relaxation of defensive tension and of the atmosphere of danger and struggle from which these structures arose. Look at Italy from 1930 to 1935. I think it would represent real conceptual and historical progress to get out of the habit of considering ideas such as "individualist or mass civilization" as categories to be used as evaluation criteria for an era or regime. This is a lesson I have taken from fascism which, now that it's about to fall, should not be thought of simply as a tumor that just needs to be cut out for things to go back to the way they were before. The criterion to be used today is "nationalist or cosmopolitan civilization"; and it is clear that even though both are totalitarian, the Europe of Hitler (with the caste division into Spartiates and Helots, as you so effectively characterize it) would be a nationalist civilization, while a communist Europe would represent a cosmopolitan civilization. Placing the problem of European unity at the center means having understood this shift in

---

[31] Europe, the captive, made her savage conqueror captive (Horace).

terminology. Placing "individualist civilization or mass civilization" at the center means remaining the prisoner of a pre-fascist mindset, and having practically given up on European unity.

3rd — I have no confidence whatever in the "numerous and influential" men who "speak European" in England and America. They will speak another language altogether as soon as they have ceased to be part of the opposition. England and America entered the war not to defend Europe, but to defend the European balance of power. And there is only one thing that would bring them round to an actual unification of their zone of influence — the danger of a Russo-German unification. So I think your hope that "the war will last long enough to shatter even further the internal resistance that Russia might offer to a penetration of ideas and ways of life" is a huge mistake. (Another mistake, incidentally, is that Russia has been overwhelmed in the war only because it was attacked by Germany. Just think of the Russian-Yugoslavian pact in March). The weakening of Russia would only encourage England and the United States in their reconstruction policy of creating "security zones" against the danger of Russia and Germany, in fomenting enmity between them, etc. Betting on England alone as a determining factor in European unity is letting yourself onto a slope that will lead you, without your realizing it, into playing England's imperialist game. Already, in your most recent writings, the problem of "individualist civilization and mass civilization" has taken clear precedence over the problem of European unity. And explicitly closing the door on any Russo-German solution banishes the European federation into the realm of beautiful utopias.[32]

---

[32]"I don't delude myself in the slightest that I have convinced you," Colorni continued in a paragraph that he then deleted. "But if you will allow an old friend to make another personal observation, I want to tell you that I don't like you at all in your new role as an "individualist" and advocate of "western civilization." I liked you much better when you confessed to an ill-concealed admiration for Hitler, when the reasons for your polemics against the USSR were inefficiency, pusillanimity, and refusal to fight; when what disturbed you in it was not the totalitarianism but their petty and mean politics. Now that these accusations have largely fallen apart, you have retreated into the stronghold of 'individualist civilization.' It is an environment that seems to me not at all suited to your character. It is an environment that is not very 'Pantagruelian.'"

5. Letter to the Ventotene Federalists[33]

Political Situation, Anti-fascist Parties, and Federalist Initiatives

Dear friends,

At the conclusion of a nearly plenary session it was decided that I should take over the direction of the movement. I hope to discharge my function to everyone's satisfaction. Our last discussions had caused me to fear that our shortcomings were too serious to allow us collaborate productively. But the articles you have sent, which I agree with almost completely (concerning the few points I have reservations about, all my friends here agree with me), clearly show that you also think the tone of the newspaper should be such that both our points of view are entitled to citizenship. This is the advantage of being a movement and not a political party. We can give the newspaper a generic character without going into the details of an issue. But for the main questions among ourselves we can produce mimeographed pamphlets — which I hope will be successful because they will showcase the vitality in our movement and the passion for ideas.

The leadership is constituted as follows.

Moreno[34] and Giunio[35] will work with me in the hands on editing of the newspaper. Moreno will also maintain relations with Milan, and will deal with people and parties and everything concerning the press. Giunio will be in charge of the distribution and dissemination of printed material. Turacciolino[36] will maintain contacts with you. Ostinato[37] will do the same work as Giunio. Pessimista[38] will be our

---

[33]This letter was written two months after the Allies disembarked in Tunisia, and therefore before 25 July, from Rome, where Colorni had gone after escaping from confinement at Melfi. It was addressed especially to Altiero Spinelli, who was at Ventotene at the time [note by Leo Solari].
[34]*Moreno*: Guglielmo Usellini.
[35]*Giunio*: Cerilo Spinelli.
[36]*Turacciolino*: Fiorella Spinelli.
[37]*Ostinato*: not identified.
[38]*Pessimista* [Pessimist]: Mario Alberto Rollier.

representative in Milan. Minister without portfolio, N. 2.[39] Ciccione Volante,[40] who from now on will be known as Eustacchio, will be the general secretary of the movement, working full-time. Naturally, these duties are flexible and can be shifted according to the occasion and need.

Political situation here: 1) I have recently had a long conversation with the main representative of the PUM [Proletarian Unity Movement], an old friend of mine from Milan. The PUM holds to the position of typical Marxist classist tradition. On the complete break between proletariat and bourgeoisie, absolute intransigence; they consider the AP [Action Party] to be fascism in disguise, they reject any idea of a single front, and they would rather put up with fascism a little longer than collaborate with bourgeois parties. To my objection that on their own like this they will not bring fascism down, and if they get England to do it they preclude the possibility of having any weight in the future situation, he answers that England's plans will not be altered in the least by internal events in Italy; and in any case, he argues, England's influence on the destiny of the continent will be less than one might think. He agrees that Europe will be split into two great spheres of influence and that Italy will be in the English one. He predicts that Russia will have no interest in any sphere not its own, and will actually order communists to secretly boycott the revolution. The task of the Italian proletariat will thus be to make the revolution on its own. On the issue of European unity he says to think naturally, as he always has, since this goal has always figured in his program (that is, speaking plainly, he does not think about it at all). In general, he thinks there is nothing essentially new to discover — that the terms of the struggle are still the traditional ones.

My impression: It is a party that aims to exploit the CP's [Communist Party] at least initially weak position in Italy, where they will be bound to accept English predominance and a democratic government. Thus the PUM will attract the discontented proletarian

---

[39]*N. 2*: Ursula Hirschmann.
[40]*Ciccione Volante* [Flying Fat Man]: Gigliola Spinelli.

masses to itself. He may even succeed, if the communists are not more skillful than he is — but I think they will be more skillful, and that his will never be more than one of the eternal little groups of discontented socialists. Even now it's not the only one, and these groups will never get together for reasons of personal ambition (he says so himself). They hate the bulk of the socialist party, which they call the servant of the bourgeoisie. Having said all this, however, if England (as is possible and probable) follows a policy of reconstruction in Europe and Russia has no interest in the sphere of influence not its own, a party like this, if it can wean the masses from the narcotics fed them by the communists, may serve a notable function in its explicit refusal to accept a static situation, acting as an agitator in a state of affairs that threatens to congeal into "there is nothing to be done." But certainly today, with its ostentatious leftism and blind intransigence, amounting to what might almost be called electioneering, it brings to mind the pre-1933 German communists. With us, however, they would like to collaborate; indeed we have set up negotiations which, if they go well, may offer us an easy way to print our material. The basic idea here is that we will collaborate with anybody if there is mutual benefit favoring the underground work. This is essential if we want to accomplish anything; and we would ask that you do the same, eliminating personal friction as much as possible. Therefore, in spite of your prohibition, we will send you their answer to their comrades there; indeed, we request that you announce to them the forthcoming arrival of this answer and that you put yourselves at their complete disposal concerning the contacts they may need. You absolutely must do this — they have done us so many favors up to now (for example, they have greatly facilitated my stay here) that it would be downright ugly to refuse them this small service.

2) *CP*: After the dissolution of the Communist International it essentially split into two groups: the 1st of these, which still takes orders from Moscow and is for the largest support base — the king, the pope, anyone really, seeks only the destruction of fascism, peace, and participation in the future government. This last point is an essential condition for its support. Negotiations are underway

in Milan for a united front composed of: Reconstruction, AP, socialists, social-Christians, and communists. The MUP has refused to participate. This group of official communists now also includes some very well educated young intellectuals, some of whom are of the first rank, who without any experience or political preparation entered the party out of activist enthusiasm, considering this the party where there is the most to do (work among the masses, strikes, etc.). For now they are enthusiastic and extremely disciplined, but they make no mystery of their theoretical reservations (one of them spoke freely to me of the future task of intellectuals to combat "Marxist ignorance") and do not rule out leaving the party the day they are no longer satisfied with it. They seem to represent a rather new type of communist functionary. Who knows if they'll let the party "squeeze" them or if they'll break away from it, or if the party will let them go on as they are. The 2nd group is the group of old communists who, for one reason or another, have lost contact with the center in Moscow; still seeing themselves as the truest interpreters of the Communist International, they want class politics and lean toward collaborating with the MUP. If I'm not mistaken, their position would be something like the position of "Gatto[41] and La Volpe[42]" there where you are. Overall, the first group seem more interesting to me. I will see if I can make contact with them.

3) The AP, after the recent arrests, is in a period of chaos. But I'm afraid you are kidding yourselves about this party as such. We can work very successfully among its followers (and we do so fairly profitably). But its most responsible leaders (I talked a long time with one of them before his arrest) do not believe in European unity at all, nor that England can be an initiator of it. Indeed, they think the English capable of throwing the AP itself overboard and casting their lot with the monarchy and the army (but see the latest news). It seems that the Anglo-Saxons do not have excessive confidence in the Italian exiles and do not treat them very well. They refuse (it would appear) to appoint a nominal government committee,

---

[41] *Gatto* [Cat]: Camilla Ravera.
[42] *La Volpe* [The Fox]: Umberto Terracini.

even in view of the invasion. This is evidently for fear of a repeat of Giraud-De Gaulle-Darlan, and because they don't want to tie their hands concerning how they will organize Italy after the war. You will say that this news is slanted; I merely pass it to you as it was given to me. We have excellent relations with the Action Party, as indeed we do with all the parties (except with the official CP, with whom we have no relations for now) and several of our members are members of the AP. For their part, however, there is some suspicion of us and a certain fear that we are deliberately causing disruption in their ranks in order to take away members. Therefore the stipulation that we are "a movement and not a party" is as timely and necessary as ever. Next to the MUP there is also a UP, which has a similar program and with which we also have relations.

I have just now had an interview with an exponent from abroad[43] (France) of the so-called "Action Committee," a single front, established in France since 1941, consisting of communists, Justice and Liberty, and socialists from the Nenni and Saragat group. This person is clearly close to the communists and has promised to put us in contact with the CP center in Milan (he is also my old friend). This action committee included, for JL, first Trentin, then Lussu, who is now in Europe, and apparently also Magrini [and] Cianca, who is presently in Algeria; it had notable resonance in France among the emigrant masses. In Italy it was not widely known. Here it has now been replaced by the united front whose formation I have already spoken to you about. We will certainly try and join this united front and participate in it. It is a united front for immediate action to bring down fascism before the end of the war. In it, the AP complains about the communists, whose channels are too broad and who would form alliances with anybody. Obviously, the AP is worried about protecting its image as a non right-wing party and about possibly compromising contacts. Likewise, the communists complain about the AP, which is reluctant to take concrete action and wants to limit itself to a press campaign. The communists, on the other hand, would like to begin an action of the kind the De Gaullists carry out in France, initially against the Germans in Italy. I

---

[43] Not identified.

am also of the opinion that we are at the point where we need to start to act. Moreno, who is going to Milan soon, will make contact with this united front and try to join it officially.

About two months ago, at the time of the fall of Tunisia, the question of a coup d'état was current for some weeks. Senators and generals went to the king. The king took refuge behind his constitutional position — that is, behind the vote supporting the government in the House and the Senate. (In fact, the argument is not valid, because the head of government is responsible today only to the king). It seems, in fact, that the king is highly devoted to Mussolini and decided not to let go of him. Various generals commanding army units spoke with representatives of the underground parties. They stated that they were ready to act if the masses took the initiative. The party representatives promised the support of the masses once the generals moved. So each was waiting for the other and everything stayed the way it was. Apparently ammunition is being taken from army units inside the country to be given to the militia. It seems that for now the movement has quieted down. The princess of Piedmont is hugely active in the anti-fascist group.

Very latest news: Since the landing. Radio London has announced the formation of a National Front, composed of socialists, communists, AP and social Christians, aimed at the formation of a democratic republic. This means that negotiations with the king failed once and for all before the landing. This will greatly increase the activity of the AP.

Our work here: The 2nd issue of the newspaper will be out shortly, and will include an initial brief on the action, your article on Churchill's speech, an article entitled "Movement or Party," an article on the dissolution of the Communist International, your critique of the AP program.

Please send us more articles of the kind that you have already sent. And Pantagruel,[44] you should also send me a new answer to my first letter, which could be published in a mimeographed pamphlet.

---

[44] *Pantagruel*: Altiero Spinelli.

We would like to publish the entire conversation. In this answer, you could include the criticism of the myth of German revolution and your observations on the links between totalitarianism and collectivism, but modify the tone and make it more presentable. I also enclose my answer to this letter. I would like you to let some friends who are there read my first letter — namely, Gatto and La Volpe, Ondeggiante,[45] Metafisico,[46] the one who had you send the poster to MUP,[47] Romanziere,[48] Biondo Ossigenato,[49] and Violinista[50] (La Volpe's roommate).

Please confirm the arrival of the box immediately.

Attachments: Letter to Pipeta's[51] friend, accompanied by N. 2 (Pipeta's letter hasn't arrived yet). Commodo's answer to Pantagruel.

Commodo (Aldo from now on)

---

[45] *Ondeggiante*: Francesco Fancello.
[46] *Metafisico* [Metaphysician]: Riccardo Bauer.
[47] Sandro Pertini.
[48] *Romanziere* [Novelist]: Alberto Jacometti.
[49] *Biondo Ossigenato* [Bleached Blond]: Giuseppe Paganelli.
[50] *Violinista* [Violinist]: Mauro Scoccimarro.
[51] *Pipeta*: Manlio Rossi-Doria.

6. Letter to Ernesto Rossi[52]

The Politics of Federalism as a Movement

5 August, evening [1943]

Dear Ernesto,

[...]

One. I think that from now on we must not present ourselves solely as a cultural movement whose purpose is to spread the federalist idea among its groups, but as a political organization offering well-defined ideas. The fall of fascism marks the beginning of an era in which European unity ceases to be a distant ideal, but takes the form of an attainable possibility, and this means that we have to be present in concrete day-to-day political life, actively showing that the words of the directive of European unity are the most alive, most readily grasped and most directly felt as responsive to the situation. This does not mean that we have to be a party, because we do not need to produce a demanding program of policies, domestic, social, etc., and because we can tolerate within our ranks different viewpoints on these problems; another reason is that the task we set ourselves is not necessarily to take power, but essentially to act in such a way as to promote or bring about situations in international politics that move in the direction of European unity. Our job now should no longer be so much one of persuasion, but rather of real political action, making use of all the tools of politics (propaganda among the masses, action in party leadership centres, contacts with foreign movements, diplomacy, the use of 'myths' and popular 'magic words', etc.).

Two. Having said this, a crucial question presents itself: should

---

[52]This letter was sent to Ernesto Rossi in preparation for the conference held in Milan later in August 1943. It asks whether the European Federalists should built a Party or develop a Movement. And whether, if they become a Movement, they should act by themselves or through existing political parties. The solution would prove to be the latter; and Eugenio would make note of it.

our actions be carried out within the various parties, or should we turn directly to the masses in our own name? It is difficult to resolve this question under present conditions. But to be clear, we have to bear in mind that none of the present-day parties, from the AP [Action Party] to the Communists, have so far made direct contact with the masses, who have been effectively de-politicized by fascism. For now, everyone has a clientele consisting of old pre-fascist politicians and people who have been working underground. But the real masses, who for years and years really believed that democracy and socialism were tired relics of the past (this is the only belief that fascism has succeeded in inculcating in everyone, even the workers) – the real masses, how will they react to the actions of the various current parties? Won't they be put off, nauseated by the tired phrases the parties produce? Won't they be much more ready to accept the word of European unity, as long as it is perceived concretely — that is, as addressing the present, urgent problem to be solved, without too many institutional and social trappings? I think so: and in the few experiences I've had up to now in 'virgin' environments, I've felt an immediate response to our words that was much more alive and understanding than in the 'crafty' atmosphere of politics. If this impression should prove correct, it would be a good idea to set up our activities so as to appeal directly to the masses, and not through the brokering of the various existing parties.

If on the other hand my impression is wrong, then it would be better to act within the various parties: not so much by putting forward a federalist program as by pushing them a little at a time to assume attitudes and goals in their political activities that we consider appropriate for the purposes of European unity. Therefore, we should move to occupy leadership positions within them; and of course not only in the Action Party, but also in the Socialist Party at least, seeing as we will never get into the Communist Party.

[...]

7. Letter to Federalist Friends in Switzerland[53]

Political-military Situation, Political Parties, and Federalist Movement

November 1943

Dear all,

We haven't heard anything more about you or what you are doing, except the news that you're in Switzerland. Moreno[54] got out some days ago; since he would have scant possibility for movement and action here, we decided together that he should come to you, bringing with him as much news as possible. We are hoping that Giunio[55] will also be able to get out within days, using the same method as Moreno. I will now try and explain to you as clearly as possible what things are like here in Rome. I say here in Rome, because contact with Northern Italy is scarce and sporadic; and in any case my impression is that the political configuration in Italy over the next months will be decided when the English get to Rome.

The political-military situation. There are not a great many Germans in Rome, and so far they haven't carried out excessive acts of terror, apart from the deportation of the Jews, which was truly brutal. Evidently they are afraid of the Vatican and the various foreign embassies. They constantly circulate the rumor that all healthy men will be picked up, urging them to come forward voluntarily, but hardly anyone does. The city is full of people who live in a state of illegality (officers who failed to report, wanted politicians, men who have escaped from work service, etc.), but they circulate undisturbed and are not stopped in the street. The police have come looking for people at their homes (Pantagruel[56] and Giunio, for example, three times), but almost reluctantly, without pressure or excessive

---

[53]Letter published in Solari, L. (1980), 149–56.
[54]Guglielmo Usellini.
[55]Cerilo Spinelli.
[56]Altiero Spinelli.

searching. Telephones are not tapped, even though everybody says they are. The Ovra[57] is not operating. On the other hand, there are numerous fascist informers and many Gestapo agents who are operating, but they carry out their research in Badoglio's military circles rather than in ours. Nevertheless, many arrests have been made in our ranks as well (Petronio[58] and Sara,[59] for example, and several others with them, but no excessively serious charges were filed). The police, the PAI [Police of Italian Africa], the fascists and the Germans operate with a certain amount of independence from one another. Nevertheless, all the authorities are totally compliant with the Germans, who give them whatever they ask for; and there are truly scandalous cases of criminal cowardice. The fascists are utterly miserable. Most of them are school children 16–18 years old, and they lack the courage even to mount provocations. Even the Germans despise them. They had announced big demonstrations for October 28th, and our teams were all set to react. But at the last moment, by order of the Germans, they didn't show up, so throughout the day we didn't see a single fascist in the streets, nor a flag on the balconies. They say the fascist squads have been dissolved and Pollastrini has been arrested and removed. They also talk about a falling out between Pollastrini, head of the fascist squads, and Tamburini, the police chief, who refused to put up with the fascists replacing the police. The result of all this is that the political parties are able to act with a certain facility, in spite of the difficulties and dangers. There is in any case vastly more political life than there was under fascism, even very recently. And there is a combative atmosphere that leads people to confront the dangers with relative cheerfulness. The underground newspapers are buzzing, the streets are full of anti-German and anti-fascist graffiti that the police are unable to erase completely, and each of us has a constant sense of solidarity from the entire population.

---

[57] Organization for Vigilance and Repression of Anti-Fascism.
[58] Sandro Pertini.
[59] Giuseppe Saragat.

Military action by the political parties. Throughout the Badoglio period the political parties were unable to get anything from the military. They therefore found themselves totally unarmed at the moment of the armistice and, still worse, without organized teams that would have allowed them to participate in the struggle. All the same, some things were done, albeit chaotically and with no luck. Amid the total disintegration of the army there was a feeling that the message of the anti-fascist movements had a strong grip on the masses; and mainly we saw what should have been done but hadn't. From 8 September on, we began working feverishly to avoid ending up in the same state of impotence when the next clampdown came; the first thing was the organization of the teams. This task has occupied all the organizational activity of the three parties on the left (AP, SP, and CP), who have joined together in a "leftist bloc" in the Liberation Committee. What the prospects might be of this effort succeeding, even I — though I'm in it up to my neck — can hardly say. Certainly there has been notable progress right from the start. Many teams have been put together, the tripartite commands (that is, of the parties together) work well both downtown and in the suburbs; we can mobilize the teams quite rapidly; some actions have already been executed. But the most serious obstacle, one the whole organization has to deal with, is the lack of weapons. I think the three parties will be able to gather perhaps about two thousand men in the teams; but less than half of these are armed, and badly. How are these teams used? For the time being, only actions against the fascists are advisable and only these are carried out (especially against fascist spies). Actions against the Germans are allowed only when they leave no trace, because otherwise there would be reprisals that were too serious. What we mainly aim for are acts of sabotage. Many of these are planned and prepared; few are carried out. In preparation for an eventual state of emergency the city has been divided into eight zones, and these into sectors. The operating unit is a nucleus composed of three teams of 5 men each. A team has to stay together or be able to assemble quickly during an emergency under the zone command, jointly held by three commanders from the three parties, who will live in the same house. The actions to be carried out will be responses to possible looting, assaults on arms stores or food stores, possible actions of harassment against the German rearguards (apart from retreating troops moving through the city), and above all, during the interval between the departure of the Germans and the arrival of the English, the occupation of strategic points and important buildings, and the maintenance of public order, so that when they arrive they will find the city in the hands of party forces. There is a tripartite center (composed of Metafisico[60] for the AP, Giorgio[61] for the Cs, and for the Ss, Petronio, replaced since being arrested by the person we had gone to see that day at the Villa Borghese cafe when there were no seats, whom we'll call Ulpiano[62] from now on). Then there's a local Roman tripartite command and eight tripartite zone commands. There are also numerous militias, mainly out towards Tivoli and the Castelli.

Political positions of the various parties. The Liberation Committee is composed of 6 members: Liberals (represented by Casati), Labor Democrats (Bonomi and Ruini), Christian Democrats (De Gasperi), Action Party (Lama[63]), Socialist Party (Pietro[64]), and Communist Party (Annunciatore delle Castagne[65]). The last three of these are united in the "leftist bloc"; there is also a unity of action pact between the last two. Nevertheless, the activity of the Liberation Committee consists of nothing more than a continual tug of war between the three parties on the right and those on the left concerning anti-monarchic and republican prejudices. On 16 October a motion was finally passed that seemed to bind the rightists definitively to the anti-monarchist position, but a short time later they themselves interpreted the motion in a way that left all possibilities open. What weakens the left in this action is the attitude of the communists, who are extremely accomodating, and the other two parties' fear that they will be isolated in the Liberation Committee. Nobody has the courage to take responsibility for the break; so we move forward with this behind-the-scenes diagreement that will come to the fore the moment the English arrive. What will

---

[60] Riccardo Bauer.
[61] Giorgio Amendola.
[62] Giuliano Vassalli.
[63] Ugo La Malfa.
[64] Pietro Nenni.
[65] [Herald of the Chestnuts]: Scoccimarro.

happen then? There are two scenarios.

1) The parties on the left will successfully present a situation in the city in which they are its arbiters, completely undermining the authority of Badoglio and the king in the eyes of the English so as to get them removed (I am told that Badoglio has had little success so far in attempting to put together an army); in which case all six parties will come to power in a sort of six-person "Public Safety Committee" that will assume the royal prerogatives.

2) Alternatively, the English will leave the power with the monarchy, probably with a regency, in which case the three parties on the right will surely come to power; and what will those on the left do? The communists will do all they can to drag the other two into collaborating; but if they fail in this the communists too will be shut out and will be in serious trouble with Russia, which evidently expects them to be part of the government. If on the other hand they are able to drag the AP and the SP into a government, these three parties will split up, and the groups on the left will leave the fold and form a new left opposition party that will also include the dissident groups I will discuss shortly. This will seriously embarrass the collaborationist parties, especially the communists; indeed they are already lashing out against this idea, accusing anyone who favors it of being an agent provocateur, a traitor, etc.

There are three parties that do not participate in the Liberation Committee: the dissident communists, social-Christians and republicans. They all would have liked to be part of the Committee, but they ran up against the opposition of their corresponding parties within the committee (respectively, the communists, Christian democrats and republicans [AP]). Now they have formed their own "Republican Federation" where they have 'no responsibility', and can therefore allow themselves the luxury of speaking frankly and conducting more straightforward and even-handed politics (regarding the Moscow conference, for example). But some doubt remains whether this is not due to resentment at not being able to enter the Liberation Committee. Of course, this group is engaged in a bitter struggle against the LC, and advocates its breakup. Certainly in the AP and SP there are also powerful groups that favor this breakup — but I can't say much about people in the AP, because our friends there are very tight-lipped, presenting things as if the party were in complete agreement about the intransigence of the republicans. In the SP there is a group of young people who hold all the strings of the organization. This group (mostly from the MUP and led by Ulpiano) contains some clever and interesting elements, although their formulations are still a little awkward. Their main concern is to attract to themselves all the elements of the left that are unhappy with CP. So they are on excellent terms with the dissident groups of the Republican Federation, hoping to annex them one day in bulk; and they would favor the immediate break up of the LC. I have been fully supporting their position, but I do not feel I can fully support their mentality, which still seems mired in preconceptions. They are in any case one of the more interesting groups; they are open to new ideas, and will be the backbone of tomorrow's left. They are all definitely federalists.

Federalist movement. Let me say that Breitarme's[66] accusations are completely justified. On 9 September I found myself, with only Breitarme and Eustachio, having to mobilize our forces for action. I put together a small team composed of about twenty people (the young people from the meetings that you attended as well), which functioned fairly well over those two days, doing what little it was possible to do. This team was associated with the SP, which I had joined as soon as I came back from Milan. In the following weeks it was clear to everyone that the problem of the teams was the most urgent, with the prospect of the British arriving in only a few days, and since my team, composed largely of Jews, had in the meantime broken up, and also because work with the teams required a serious level of organization, I decided to spend my time working with the teams in the SP. I was assigned a zone, which I still have, and Eustachio and I applied ourselves to various relevant initiatives. I was so involved in this work that I had no opportunity to engage with politics. But *quod differtur non aufertur,* and now, for around the last 10 days, and with the departure of our two comrades, the time has come to initiate some more specifically political action. With this in mind I have requested permission to give only half days to working

---

[66] Braccialarghe.

in the zone, and I will seek to join the editors of *Avanti!*

I think it's very important that a federalist newspaper should be released now. It shouldn't be so much a battle flag (like so many of the papers that come out now), but rather contemplative, looking at the big picture a bit more and studying Europe's general prospects rather than focusing attention on the Liberation Committee and whether or not it will come to power. The position it takes should in my view concern the following: Today's challenge is of course to work toward the expulsion of the Germans (and we are in fact committing everything to this), but this campaign is not an end in itself. Both the communists and the AP, precisely because they are linked in their ideas to two of the powers in conflict, forget that the point of the struggle is to be ready for the European revolution that will break out in a matter of months. The problem of power should not be posed as one of monarchy vs republic (although of course you can't share power with the monarchy), but rather in terms of whether joining the government offers a way of leading the country with a firm hand in the European crisis accompanying the fall of Germany. This is the compass that we have to follow — not simply the institutional question. In other words, it is possible that even in a republic it might be advisable that the left not be in the government. Power under an English occupation would necessarily mean following an English policy line, and taking weak or strong positions in decisive moments exactly to the extent that this suited the English. Remember, the only card in a losing country's hand is the insurrection card, and we have to get ourselves ready to play it. Naturally we don't say these things to the newspapers, but this is the political line I think we should follow.

Are we up to doing what we propose? I can't guarantee it, because we don't have much in the way of forces available to us. But now with Giunio's help, I hope that for a federalist action we can bring in the federalists of the AP, who are swamped with work for their party. I can only promise you that I will give it every bit of my good will.

Warmest regards.

Angelo

8. LETTER-REPORT TO ALTIERO SPINELLI AND ERNESTO ROSSI

Report on Action Within the Socialist Party in Rome and on Publishing the Federalist Manifesto

February 13, 1944

Dear Altiero and Ernesto,

I'm writing to give you a report on recent events because I don't feel much like writing tonight. Since the day of the landings, the work of the teams has of course intensified. On the one hand we use assault teams, and on the other we're preparing a mass action for the first crucial days and for the interregnum period between the Germans and the English. The National Liberation Committee has a very tepid attitude toward the monarchy; they propose to form a provisional municipality in the interregnum period, but they lack the courage to form a temporary government. And in Bari, as you know, they didn't dare demand anything beyond the abdication of the king, meaning implicitly that they would be ready to join a government with Umberto. All the young people in all three parties on the left (AP, SP, and CP) are unhappy with bland and accommodating politics of this kind, and they let it be known quite clearly. It is likely that the parties will end up coming into a government with the monarchy, and if this happens I think the young people will all break away and form a large new opposition party. And many of them also belong to parties that are outside the NLC (dissident communists, republicas, social-Christians, etc.) and are entirely opposed to a backroom deal with the monarchy. In the SP this disagreement has broken out more violently than in the other parties. The young people (here in Rome a group notable for their intelligence and education) have formed a political committee and have fought openly against the party leadership. There have been dramatic moments when we came within a hair of expulsions, but now things seem to have been smoothed over. The day before yesterday the leadership approved an order of business in which they openly repudiated the Bari policy. This really got on the nerves of the CP and the AP, who are seen to be in a sense losing the initiative.

Giunio and Giovanni and I have been very active in this group, but within the group we advocate staying in the party for now, and not giving up on the work of the teams. In fact, we are now on the very high-risk team commanded by Giunio. I have been assigned an editorial post with *Avanti!,* and it is not unlikely that in the next shuffle they'll put me on the executive board. Throughout this uproar we have continued to argue that the problem of the NLC. and the monarchy is nothing but a pretext, and that the real, deeper disagreement is over whether the party should take on the task of simply muddling along administering the country in the difficult years that follow the war, or whether it should instead move in a revolutionary direction in the European crisis that will break out when Germany collapses. Naturally the federalist issue has been constantly at the forefront of this debate. Working with this group we started a party school, which operated with great success. There were five courses: general principles of socialism, general theory of the state, political ecomomy and Marxism, ideologies and political parties, and critical analysis of various revolutions. We will go on with this school as soon as the British arrive, preparing handouts for the courses, and I will be entrusted with organizing the popular university. None of the young people in our group are orthodox Marxists, and they are thus quite open to a revision of the principles of socialism in the direction that you propose. I have the impression, however, that the situation of the SP outside Rome, and especially in Turin and Milan, is much worse than here, indeed all but a failure.

We have published your writings in a very elegant little book that will be out within three or four days, and I enclose a draft of the frontispiece. I had to write the preface myself because we couldn't get a copy of the *Manifesto* that you published in Milan. We will sell the first 500 numbered copies at 100 lire each to sponsors, even before the English arrive, and after their arrival the other 2500 copies will go on the market at 30 lire each. We are expecting a great success. The authors will get 15% of the sales of the 2500 non-numbered copies; we figure they will give the movement the numbered copies as a gift. The cost of the printing was 27,000 lire. We are now nearing completion of a facility that will enable us to print our own and other newspapers. (The plant belongs exclusively to the European Federalist Movement). For our paper we have all the material ready, but I don't think it's too important that we bring it out now in this clandestine period teeming with pamphlets, since it would look like just one among many and we would have serious problems with distribution. Especially since your book will be much more effective propaganda. I think instead that we ought to get ready to bring something out every two weeks in the form of a Fascist Critique, as soon as the British get here, but I do not know if we'll manage this because our forces are few and money is scarce.

 The collaboration between Giunio, Giovanni and me is working better than we could have imagined. We are very close, and we complement each other. Send news. We've read a letter from Pantagruel and Pessimista and one from Pietro's brother-in-law; that's all we know about you. I also send greetings from Giunio, who is out of Rome on a mission.

 Aldo

9. Report on Federalist Activities to Altiero Spinelli and Ernesto Rossi

Federalist activity: Most of this activity took the form of an initative that G.[67] will tell you about and which could have provided us ample breathing space, even from the financial viewpoint. It had been fully launched and had begun to work successfully, when there was a blunder. We still hope that all has not been lost.

The booklet has been remarkably successful and everywhere rated as the best thing to come out in recent times. It's biggest success was in the Action Party and among the Social Christians — among those, that is, who are engaged in building a socialist ideology free of Marxist myths. The liberals also received it favorably, though with some measure of reserve. In the socialist camp, on the other hand, it was greeted with suspicion in leadership circles, like a book by an adversary.

The request for a delegation for the Federalist Congress[68] was accepted only by the Christian-social delegates who delegated Moreno[69] and the Republicans who delegated Cipriano. The socialists have said that they do not fully understand what the movement is; if it is something like "secular patronage" then they tip their hat but do not want to participate; if it is indeed serious, they fear it's a pawn in the British game. I had prepared a proxy letter containing a commitment not to characterize the federation as anti-Russian or even as an extra-Russian bloc; but they did not accept it. Instead, they are going to send Rodolfo[70] as an observer, whose task will be to report back. The liberals have done the same, and will send the old master

---

[67]G.: Giunio: Cerilo Spinelli. "The second issue of Socialist Revolution," recalled Leo Solari (1964, 41), "like some issues of Avanti, Italia Libera, Risorgimento Liberale, and Europa Unita, were printed by a clandestine printing press organized by Eugenio Colorni with the help of the Socialist Youth Federation, a press that was subsequently discovered and invaded by agents of the PAI [Police of Italian Africa] and the Police."
[68]The Assembly of European Liberation Movements, which had already met in March 1944 and had planned additional sessions.
[69]Moreno: Guglielmo Usellini.
[70]Rodolfo Morandi.

Empirico.[71] I do not know yet if it will be possible to send official letters on these assignments; but consider [. . .] my indications as formal invitations.

I was going to bring out a little magazine here. I do not know if we can manage it. In any case, we've already made a commitment to collaborate regularly with a newspaper that will most likely be entitled "Europe" and, while not an organ of the EFM, will have decidedly federalist leanings and will have on board many young members of the SP and the AP.

The Social Christians have asked to join the movement en masse. We have said they can join one at a time. We are now putting together an expanded leadership committee that will include (as individuals not officially representing parties) a Republican (Breitarme[72]), an AP member (Ostinato or Pipeta[73]), a Social Christian, and a Liberal, along with the executive committee that has operated up to now, composed of Giunio, Luisa,[74] and myself (all three from the SP).

I wanted to send you news of the political situation, but I don't have time due to the incident that occurred. I will do so if, as I foresee, G. doesn't leave tonight.

Regards
E.

May 11, 1944

---

[71] Luigi Einaudi.
[72] Giorgio Braccialarghe.
[73] Ostinato has not been identified, Pipeta is Manlio Rossi-Doria.
[74] Giunio: Cerilo Spinelli; Luisa: Luisa Villani Usellini.

Bibliography

AA.VV. (1963) *Documenti inediti dell'archivio Angelo Tasca. La rinascita del socialismo italiano e la lotta contro il fascismo dal 1934 al 1939*. Ed. Stefano Merli. Milano: Feltrinelli.
AA.VV. (2004) *Eugenio Colorni 1944–2004. Dalla guerra alla Costituzione europea*. Ed. Maria Pia Bumbaca. Roma: Municipio III.
AA.VV. (2009) "I documenti su Eugenio Colorni conservati nell'Archivio Centrale dello Stato." Ed. Giulia Vassallo. *Eurostudium 3 w,* April-June.
AA.VV. (2010) *Eugenio Colorni dall'antifascismo all'europeismo socialista e federalista*. Ed. Maurizio degl'Innocenti. Manduria-Bari-Roma: Lacaita.
AA.VV. (2011a) *Eugenio Colorni e la cultura italiana tra le due guerre*. Ed. Geri Cerchiai and Giovanni Rota. Manduria-Bari-Roma: Lacaita.
AA.VV. (2011b) *Eugenio Colorni federalista*. Ed. Fabio Zucca. Manduria-Bari-Roma: Lacaita.
Albertini, M. (1985) "Introduzione" to Altiero Spinelli, *Il progetto*.
Appadurai, A. (1996) *Modernity at Large. Cultural Dimensions of Globalization*. Minneapolis: U of Minnesota P.
Bassetti, P. (2015) *Svegliamoci Italici!* Venezia: Marsilio.
Cerchiai, G. (2009) "Introduzione" to Eugenio Colorni, *La malattia*.
___ and G. Rota. (2011) "Introduzione" to AA.VV, *Eugenio Colorni e la cultura*.
Colorni, E. (1934) "Prefazione," "Nota bio-bibliografica," and "Esposizione antologica del sistema leibniziano," Goffredo Guglielmo Leibniz, *La Monadologia*.
___ (1975) *Scritti*. Ed. N. Bobbio. Firenze: La Nuova Italia.
___ (1980) "Pagine di Eugenio Colorni," in Solari, L., *Eugenio Colorni*.
___ (1998) *Il coraggio dell'innocenza*. Ed. L. Meldolesi. Napoli: La Città del Sole.
___ (2009) *La malattia della metafisica. Scritti filosofici e autobiografici*. Ed. Geri Cerchiai. Torino: Einaudi.
___ (2016) *Microfondamenta*. Ed. Luca Meldolesi. Soveria Mannelli: Rubbettino.
___ (2017a) *La scoperta del possibile. Scritti politici*. Ed. Luca Meldolesi. Soveria Mannelli: Rubbettino.
___ (2017b) *Critical Thinking in Action. Excerpts from Political Writings and Correspondence*. Ed. Luca Meldolesi and Nicoletta Stame. Soveria Mannelli: Rubbettino.
___ (2019) *Critical Thinking in Action. Excerpts from Political Writings and Correspondence I*. Ed. Luca Meldolesi and Nicoletta Stame. New York: Bordighera Press.
___ and L. Luzzatto. (1937) "Due lettere di compagni socialisti dall'Italia." *Stato Operaio* (August).
___ and A. Spinelli. (2018) *I dialoghi di Ventotene*. Ed. Luca Meldolesi. Soveria Mannelli: Rubbettino.
Coppa, C. (2012) *La ricerca socio-economica come scoperta: Albert Hirschman e Eugenio Colorni*. Ed. Mita Marra. Napoli. Giannini editore.

d'Aquino, N. (2014) *La rete italica. Idee per un Commonwealth. Ragionamenti con e su Piero Bassetti*. Roma: Ide. 2nd updated edition, 2017.
Degl'Innocenti, M. (2010) "Introduzione a Eugenio Colorni," AA.VV., *Eugenio Colorni dall'antifascismo*.
Geertz, C. (1999) *Mondo globale, mondi locali. Cultura e politica alla fine del ventesimo secolo*. Bologna: Il Mulino.
Gerbi, S. (1999) *Tempi di malafede. Una storia italiana tra fascismo e dopoguerra. Guido Piovene e Eugenio Colorni*. Torino: Einaudi.
Graglia, P. S. (1993) "Introduzione" to Altiero Spinelli, *Machiavelli nel secolo XX*.
___ (2005) "Il socialismo federalista di Eugenio Colorni." AA.VV., *Storia e percorsi del federalismo. L'eredità di Carlo Cattaneo*. Ed. Daniela Preda and Cinzia Rognoni Vercelli, vol. 2, Bologna: Il Mulino.
___ (2010) "Colorni, Spinelli e il federalismo europeo." Degl'Innocenti, ed., *Eugenio Colorni*.
Gui, F. (2010) "Colorni 'elemento di contestazione e di cerniera' nei documenti dell'Archivio centrale dello stato." in AA.VV., *Eugenio Colorni dall'antifascismo*.
Hegel, G. W. F. (1977) *Phenomenology of the Spirit*. Oxford: Clarendon.
Hirschman, A. O. (1945) *National Power and the Structure of Foreign Trade*. Berkeley, CA: U of California P.
___ (1958) *The Strategy of Economic Development*. New Heaven, CT: Yale UP.
___ (1963) *Journeys toward Progress. Studies of Economic Policy-Making in Latin America*. New York: Twentieth Century Fund.
___ (1970) *Exit, Voice, and Loyalty: Responses to Decline in Firms, Organizations and States*. Cambridge, MA: Harvard UP.
___ (1971) *A Bias for Hope. Essays on Development and Latin America*. New Haven, CT: Yale UP.
___ (1977) *The Passions and the Interests. Political Arguments for Capitalism before Its Triumph*. Princeton, NJ: Princeton UP.
___ (1978) "Beyond Asymmetry: Critical Notes on Myself as a Young Man and Some Other Old Friends." *International Organization* (Winter); now in Albert O. Hirschman (1981), *Essays in Trespassing*.
___ (1981) *Essays in Trespassing: Economics to Politics and Beyond*. Cambridge UK: Cambridge UP.
___ (1984) "A Dissenter's Confession: Revisiting The Strategy of Economic Development." AA.VV., *Pioneers in Economic Development*. Ed. Gerald M. Meier and Dudley Seers. Oxford: Oxford UP.
___ (1987) "Io, detective dell'economia fascista." Speech of acceptance of an honorary degree from the Political Science Faculty of the University of Torino, Torino, 12 November; now in Hirschman, A. O. (1990), *Tre continenti*.
___ (1990) *Tre continenti. Economia politica e sviluppo della democrazia in Europa, Stati Uniti e America Latina*. Ed. L. Meldolesi. Torino: Einaudi.
___ (1991) *Rhetoric of Reaction. Perversity, Futility, Jeopardy*. Cambridge, MA: Harvard UP.
___ (1993) *Passaggi di frontiera*. Roma: Donzelli editore; English tr. Hirschman A.O. 1998, Ch. 3.
___ (1995) *A Propensity to Self-Subversion*. Cambridge, MA: Harvard UP.
___ (1998) *Crossing Boundaries. Selected Writings*. New York: Zone.

Leibniz, G. G. (1934) *La Monadologia*. Ed. Eugenio Colorni. Firenze: Sansoni.
Luzzatto, L., and E. Colorni (1937) "Due lettere di compagni socialisti dall'Italia." *Stato Operaio* (August).
Meldolesi, L. (1994) *Alla scoperta del possibile. Il mondo sorprendente di Albert O. Hirschman*. Bologna: il Mulino; English translation: Notre Dame: U of Notre Dame P, 1995; Spanish translation: México: Fondo de Cultura Econòmica, 1997.
___ (1998) "Introduzione. Colorni per tutti." E. Colorni, *Il coraggio*.
___ (2004) "Intervento." AA.VV., *Eugenio Colorni 1944-2004*.
___ (2010) "Eugenio Colorni and Albert Hirschman in Trieste (1937-38)." AA.VV., *Eugenio Colorni dall'antifascismo*.
___ (2012) *Federalismo possibile. Per liberare lo Stato dallo statalismo e i cittadini dall'oppressione*. Bologna: ESD.
___ (2013) *Imparare ad imparare. Saggi di incontro e di passione all'origine di una possibile metamorfosi*. Soveria Mannelli: Rubbettino.
___ (2014) *L'ultimo Hirschman e l'Europa*. Soveria Mannelli: Rubbettino. Spanish translation: Buenos Aires: Universidad Nacional de Quilmes, 2018.
___ (2015) *Italici e città*. Roma.
___ (2016a) *Rammendare il mondo*. Soveria Mannelli: Rubbettino.
___ (2016b) *Intransigenze, Mediterraneo e democrazia*. Soveria Mannelli: Rubbettino.
Merli, S. (1963) "Introduzione." AA.VV., *Documenti inediti*.
Pavone, C. (2004) "Intervento." AA.VV., *Eugenio Colorni 1944-2004*.
___ (2010) "L'incontro con Colorni." AA.VV., *Eugenio Colorni dall'antifascismo*.
Paolini, E. (1996) *Altiero Spinelli. Dalla lotta antifascista alla battaglia per la Federazione europea. 1920-1948: documenti e testimonianze*. Bologna: Il Mulino.
Pasquinucci, D. (2010) "La Prefazione al Manifesto di Ventotene." AA.VV., *Eugenio Colorni dall'antifascismo*.
Quaranta, M. (2011) "La 'scoperta' di Eugenio Colorni nelle riviste del secondo dopoguerra. Gli scritti sulla relatività." AA.VV., *Eugenio Colorni e la cultura*.
Riccardi, R. (1940) "Riorganizzazione economica europea." *Antieuropa* (September-October); now in Edmondo Paolini (1996), *Altiero Spinelli*.
Rossi, E. (1944) "Eugenio Colorni." *L'Avvenire dei lavoratori* (15 July); now in Ernesto Rossi (1975), *Un democratico*.
___ (1975) *Un democratico ribelle*. Ed. Giuseppe Armani. Parma: Guanda.
___ and A. Spinelli (1944) *Problemi della Federazione europea*. Ed. Eugenio Colorni. Roma.
Salvemini, G. (1947) "Aspetti politici della rivoluzione europea." Now in Edmondo Paolini (1996), *Altiero Spinelli*.
Senise, C. (1945) *Quando ero Capo della polizia 1940-1943*. Roma: Ruffolo editore. New edition, Mursia, 2012.
Spinelli, A. (1984) *Come ho tentato di diventare saggio. I. Io, Ulisse*. Bologna: Il Mulino.
___ (1985) *Il progetto europeo*, Bologna: Il Mulino.
___ (1993) *Machiavelli nel secolo XX. Scritti del confino e della clandestinità*. Ed. Piero Graglia. Bologna: Il Mulino.
___ and E. Rossi (1944) *Problemi della Federazione europea*. Ed. Eugenio Colorni.

Roma.
___ and E. Colorni (2018) *I dialoghi di Ventotene*. Ed. Luca Meldolesi. Soveria Mannelli: Rubbettino.
Solari, L. (1964) *I giovani di rivoluzione socialista*. Roma: iepi.
___ (1980) *Eugenio Colorni. Ieri e sempre*. Venezia: Marsilio.
___ (2004) "La lezione di Angelo." AA.VV., *Eugenio Colorni 1944-2004*, cit.
Tedesco, A. (2014) *Il partigiano Colorni e il grande sogno europeo*. Roma: Editori Riuniti.
Vassalli, G. (2004) "Intervento." AA.VV., *Eugenio Colorni 1944-2004*.
___ (2010) "Ricordo di Angelo (Eugenio Colorni e la Resistenza romana)." AA.VV., *Eugenio Colorni dall'antifascismo*.
Vassallo, G.(2009) "'Il Prof. Eugenio Colorni' nelle carte dell'Archivio Centrale dello Stato." *Eurostudium 3 w*, January-March.
Ventura, A. (2010) "Colorni e gli intellettuali italiani tra fascismo e antifascismo." AA.VV., *Eugenio Colorni dall'antifascismo*.
Vigorelli, A. (2011) "Antifascismo tra i giovani. Il caso di 'Pietre.'" AA.VV., *Eugenio Colorni e la cultura*.
Watts, R.L. (2005) "Comparing Forms of Federal Partnership." *Theories of Federalism: A Reader*. Ed. D. Karmis and W. Norman. New York: Palgrave.
Zucca, F. (2010) "Eugenio Colorni, Guglielmo Usellini e l'Unità europea." AA.VV., *Eugenio Colorni dall'antifascismo*.
___ (2011) "Introduzione." AA.VV., *Eugenio Colorni federalista*.

Index of Subjects

Administration, functionaries 48, 58–61
Anthropomorphism 112–13
Anti-fascism 17–19, 21, 24, 35, 45–47, 54, 61, 63, 67–72, 85, 147, 170, 181

Border posts 21, 80–83, 85, 90–91, 94, 95–97

Capitalism 36, 70, 73, 77–78
Center (Internal Center of the Italian Socialist Party) 14, 19, 21, 67, 69, 71, 79–82, 86, 89–91, 94, 95–97
Collectivism vs. market economy 163–67, 175
Communication and propaganda 20, 22, 79, 91–92, 174, 184–85, 189, 191

Democracy 24–25, 33, 37–38, 49, 68
Depression 26, 62, 111
Discovery 12, 17, 35, 40, 56, 121, 129
Doubts 24–29, 32, 47, 49

Education 22
Effervescence 23
Europe 27–29, 32, 41–43, 47, 49, 151, 155–67, 177–78, 188

Fascism 12, 16, 18, 25, 28, 34, 36, 46, 57, 68, 73, 76–78, 147, 155, 177
Federalism 27, 33–44, 48, 50, 51–53, 184–85
Federalist Movement 29, 33–34, 41, 44, 162, 168, 177, 184–85, 189, 191–92
Fever for action 30, 153
Freedom 45

Historical standpoint 46

Ideology 14–15, 24, 30, 32, 34, 38, 48, 153–55, 162

Imperialism 16, 28, 37, 160–61, 167
Innocence 12, 49
Leadership 14–15, 20, 33–34, 38, 45, 48, 71, 152, 155, 161, 168, 177
Literature 104, 108, 110–11, 114, 116, 118–20, 125–26, 127–36, 138–41, 150
Love 125, 136–37, 139–41, 149

Manifesto 29–30, 34–35, 188, 191
Mass struggle 20–22, 74, 92, 174, 178
Mathematics, geometry 109–11, 113, 115–16, 122, 127
Method 11, 12, 14–15, 17, 21–22, 24–26, 107–09, 111
Middle classes 14–16, 21, 68, 73
Moralist 45

Nationalism 16, 27–28, 32, 37, 39, 41–44, 47–48, 51–53, 155, 159, 161, 166–67
Nazism 12, 16, 28, 57, 59, 159, 167, 179–82, 185

Organization 19–21, 70, 79–80

Patriotism 16, 21, 46
Perspectives 31, 159–62
Philosophy 13, 30, 45, 58, 62, 103, 107–08, 112, 115, 116–18, 121–14, 126, 129, 132–34, 150, 153–54
Possibilism 11–18, 32, 56, 58, 60
 of ways out 12, 31
 of proposals 12
Psychology 107–09, 114, 117, 120, 123, 125–26, 151

Rhetoric 25
Revolution 69, 163, 168, 170, 185, 188

Science 26, 61, 106, 109, 116–17, 124, 127, 141, 150
Students 22

Socialism 13–21, 33, 37–38, 44–45, 47, 170–71, 184, 187
Social problems 47–48
Solidarity 19–20
Spontaneity 19
Struggle within the fascist context 18, 73–78
Surprise 24

Systems 103, 119, 123, 153–54

Teacher 22–23, 26, 31, 46, 188

Universalism 41–44, 47–48, 166–67

Young militants 45, 172, 184, 187–88

Index of Names

Agostini, pseudonym of Colorni Eugenio 14–15n16, 15, 18n25, 23n36, 67, 72, 83
Albertini, Mario 35n71
Aldo, pseudonym of Colorni Eugenio 23n36, 175, 189
Amendola, Giorgio 182n61
Angelo, pseudonym of Eugenio Colorni 23n36, 185
Annunciatore delle Castagne [Herald of the Chestnuts], pseudonym of Scoccimarro Mauro 182
Anselmi, pseudonym of Colorni Eugenio 23n36, 79, 83, 85, 87
Appadurai, Arjun 51n104

Bacchelli, Riccardo 135
Badoglio, Pietro 180, 181, 183
Bassetti, Piero 51n104, 51n106
Bauer, Riccardo 175n46, 182n60
Benvenuti, Giuseppe 55
Bernard, Paul 95
Berto, pseudonym of Morandi Rodolfo 14
Bianco, pseudonym of Visentini Bruno 92
Biondo Ossigenato [Bleached Blond], pseudonym of Paganello Giuseppe 175, 175n49
Bonomi, Ivanoe 182
Braccialarghe, Giorgio 29n54, 184n66, 192n72
Breitarme, pseudonym of Braccialarghe Giorgio 184, 192
Buleghin, Arturo 29n54

Cantor, Georg 111
Carducci, Giosuè 13
Casati, Alessandro 182
Castelnuovo, Guido 115
Cattaneo, Carlo 38n81, 50, 51, 52n109
Cézanne, Paul 131
Chesterton, Gilbert Keith 104, 131, 132
Chierici, Lorenzo 59
Cianca, Alberto 173
Ciancarini, Alfredo 59
Ciccione Volante [Flying Fat Man], pseudonym of Spinelli Gigliola 170, 170n40
Cipriano 191
Colorni, Alberto 57n120, 149
Colorni, Silvia Clara, daughter 27, 57, 149
Colorni, Silvia, sister 58, 112, 113, 121, 124, 149
Commodo, pseudonym of Eugenio Colorni 23n36, 175

D.4, pseudonym of Eugenio Colorni 23n36
D.5, pseudonym of Eugenio Colorni 23n36, 93
D'Aquino, Niccolò 51n104, 51n106
D'Azeglio, Massimo 106
Dante [Alighieri] 104, 110, 134
Darlan, François 173
De Broglie, Louis-Victor Pierre Raymond 109
De Gasperi, Alcide 182
De Gaulle, Charles 173
Degl'Innocenti, Maurizio 12n7, 14, 14n15, 18n24, 19n26, 19n27
Descartes, René 19n27, 93n9, 122
Di Marco, Amedeo 54n112, 60
Diderot, Denis 106
Dimitroff, Georghi 99
Disney, Walt 108

Empirico, pseudonym of Einaudi Luigi 192
Enriques, Paolo 113
Eustacchio, pseudonym of Spinelli Gigliola 170

Fancello, Francesco 175n45

199

Faravelli, Giuseppe 14, 15, 15n17, 15n18, 15n19, 15n21, 19n27, 20n31, 21, 22, 54, 54n113
Fichte, Johann Gottlieb 121
France, Anatole 132, 133
Franco, Giuseppe 103n13
Franzin, Elio 20n31
Fundo, Lazar 29n54

Galilei, Galileo 122, 133
Garbo, Greta 105
Garibaldi, Giuseppe 156
Gatto [Cat], pseudonym of Ravera Camilla 172, 172n41, 175
Geertz, Clifford 11, 35n73, 51n107
Gentile, Giovanni 13, 13n13, 58
George, Stefan 119, 120
Gerbi, Sandro 45n92, 54n113, 58, 59n123
Geymonat, Ludovico 150
Gilmartin, Michael 5
Giraud, Henri 173
Giovanni 188, 189
Giunio, pseudonym of Spinelli Cerilo 169, 169n35, 179, 185, 188, 189, 191n67, 192, 192n74
Giussani, Enrico 29n54
Goethe, Johann Wolfgang 104, 109, 110, 120, 134, 141
Graglia, Piero 29n54, 29n55, 34n68, 151n23, 165n29
Grossi, Tommaso 104
Gui, Francesco 44, 44n90, 54, 56, 58
Guida, Marcello 59

Hauptmann, Gerhardt 131
Hegel, Georg Wilhelm 56, 56n119, 121, 126
Hemingway, Ernest 135
Hirschman, Albert O. 11, 11n3, 11n4, 11n5, 12, 12n7, 13, 13n11, 14, 19n26, 20n31, 23, 24, 24n38, 24n39, 24n40, 25, 25n41, 25n42, 25n43, 26, 35, 35n73, 38n80, 38n81, 40, 40n82, 40n84, 40n85, 41n86, 42n87, 45–46, 52n110, 56, 57n121

Hirschmann, Eva 28, 149, 150
Hirschmann, Hedwig 150
Hirschmann, Otto Albert 11n3, 150
Hirschmann, Ursula 13, 13n11, 21n32, 22, 27, 27n46, 27n47, 29, 29n55, 34, 49n99, 56, 57, 57n120, 57n121, 60, 61, 62, 103, 104, 105, 106, 107, 109, 110, 111, 113, 114, 115, 117, 125n16, 145, 149, 170n39
Hitler, Adolf 13, 13n11, 28, 166, 167n32
Hölderlin, Friedrich 119, 120
Horace 166n31
Huxley, Aldous 127, 129, 130, 132, 135, 136

Ibsen, Henrik 105

Joseph, pseudonym of Faravelli Giuseppe 15n17, 15n19, 15–16n21, 19n27, 20n31, 22, 79, 85, 85n5, 85n6, 85n8, 89, 95, 99

Kafka, Franz 104, 131, 132, 141
Kant, Immanuel 118, 121, 123
Kipling, Rudyard 104, 104
Kleist, Heinrich von 119

La Malfa, Ugo 182n63
La Volpe [Fox], pseudonym of Terracini Umberto 172, 172n42, 175
Lama, pseudonym of La Malfa, Ugo 182
Lawrence, David Herbert 129, 130
Leibniz, Gottfried Wilhelm von 13, 58, 107, 110, 122
Lenin, Nicolaj 16, 71
Lentini, Sirio 45n91
Lepenies, Wolf 35n73
Leto, Guido 54, 59
Lussu, Emilio 173
Luxemburg, Rosa 16
Luzzatto, Lucio 18n25

Magrini, pseudonym of Garosci Aldo 173
Mann, Thomas 118, 119, 120, 132, 135,

141
Maro, pseudonym of Luzzatto, Lucio 18n25
Martinetti, Piero 13n12
Marx, Karl 36n76
Meldolesi, Luca 11n4, 12n8, 24n38, 24n40, 40n82, 46n93, 48n97, 50n102, 51n105, 51n106, 51n107, 52n109
Merli, Stefano 13n9, 99n11
Metafisico [Metaphysician], pseudonym of Bauer, Riccardo 175, 175n46, 182
Modigliani, Giuseppe Emanuele 99
Molière, pseudonym of Jean-Baptiste Poquelin 11
Molnar, Ferenc 131
Monnet, Jean 40n84
Morandi, Rodolfo 14, 14n46, 19, 191n70
Moreno, pseudonym of Usellini, Guglielmo 169, 169n34, 174, 179, 191, 191n69
Morpurgo Tagliabue, Guido 150
Mozart, Wolfgang Amadeus 116
Mussolini, Benito 16n22, 26, 33, 58, 59, 59n124, 75, 76, 174

N.2, pseudonym of Ursula Hirschmann 170, 170n39, 175
Nenni, Pietro 16, 44, 59, 99n11, 173, 182n64
Newton, Isaac 133
Nietzsche, Friedrich 115, 116, 118, 119, 120, 141

Olanda, pseudonym of Colorni, Eugenio 23n36
Ondeggiante, pseudonym of Fancello, Francesco 175, 175n45
Ostinato 169, 169n37, 192, 192n73

Paganelli, Giusppe 175n49
Pantagruel, pseudonym of Spinelli, Altiero 174, 174n44, 175, 179, 189

Paolini, Edmondo 28n51, 29n54, 34, 34n70, 50n102
Pasquinucci, Daniele 33n62, 34n66, 34n68
Pennetta, Epifanio 57, 57n120, 59, 60, 62, 63
Pertini, Sandro 175n47, 180n58
Perucca, Eligio 106
Peruzzi, Francesco 59, 60n128
Pessimista [Pessimist], pseudonym of Rollier, Mario Alberto 169, 169n38, 189
Petronio, pseudonym of Pertini, Sandro 180, 182
Picasso, Pablo 132
Pipeta, pseudonym of Rossi-Doria, Manlio 175, 175n51, 192, 192n73
Planck, Max 117
Plato 122, 134
Pollastrini, Guglielmo 180
Pontecorvo, family 63
Proust, Marcel 118, 141

Quaranta, Mario 11n1
Quisling, Vidkun 157, 161

Ravera, Camilla 172n41
Reichenbach, Hans 141
Riccardi, Raffaello 28n51
Rilke, Rainer Maria 138–40
Roberto, Dino 29n54
Rollier, Mario Alberto 169n38
Romanziere [Novelist], pseudonym of Jacometti, Alberto 175, 175n48
Rossi, Ernesto 27, 27n47, 28n51, 29n53, 29n55, 33, 34n68, 35, 35n71, 134, 150, 151n25, 165n29, 177, 177n52, 187, 191
Rossi-Doria, Manlio 63, 175n51, 192n73
Rubbettino, Florindo 11n1
Ruggeri, pseudonym of Colorni, Eugenio 20n31, 22, 23, 85n8, 89, 93, 95, 99, 100
Ruini, Camillo 182

Salvemini, Gaetano 50
Sara, pseudonym of Saragat, Giuseppe 180, 180n59
Saragat, Giuseppe 173, 180n59
Schelling, Friedrich Willhelm 121
Schiller, Friedrich 105
Schwarz, Clara 150
Schwarz, Laura 150
Schwarz, Susanna 150
Schwarz, Willi 149, 150
Scoccimarro, Mauro 175n50, 182n65
Senise, Carmine 57, 59, 59n124, 59n125
Sereni, Emilio 13n13, 27n49
Sereni, Enrico 13n13, 27n49
Sereni, Enzo 13n13, 27n49
Shakespeare, William 104, 105, 106, 110, 134
Sienkiewicz, Henryk 104
Skendi, Stavo 29n54
Skinner, Quentin 35n73
Slataper, Scipio 104–05, 105
Solari, Leo 11–12n6, 14–15n16, 17n23, 19n29, 45n92, 169n33, 179n53, 191n67
Sophocles 125
Spinelli, Altiero 27, 27n48, 27n50, 28n51, 29n55, 31n60, 33n61, 33n63, 34n68, 35, 35n71, 35n72, 134, 150, 151, 151n22, 151n23, 151n25, 163, 163n27, 163n28, 165n29, 165n30, 169n33, 174n44, 179n56, 187, 191
Spinelli, Cerilo 169n35, 179n55, 191n67, 192n74
Spinelli, Fiorella 169n35
Spinelli, Gigliola 170n40
St. Augustin 124
St. Thomas Aquinas 124
Stame, Nicoletta 11n1, 46

Standt 109, 110, 111, 112, 115
Steinbeck, John 131, 133
Stendhal, pseudonym of Marie-Henri Beyle 141
Stravinsky, Igor 131

Tamburini, Tullio 180
Tasca, Angelo 14, 15, 15n18, 15n21, 16, 79, 85, 86, 93, 99n11
Tedesco, Antonio 26n44, 45n91
Terracini, Umberto 172n42
Trentin, Silvio 173
Turacciolino, pseudonym of Spinelli, Fiorella 169, 169n36
Turgenev, Ivan 104–05

Ulpiano, pseudonym of Vassalli, Giuliano 182, 184
Usellini, Guglielmo 169n34, 179n54, 191n69

Van Gogh, Vincent 131
Vassalli, Giuliano 33n62, 45n92, 182n62
Vassallo, Giulia 54, 55n117, 58
Ventura, Angelo 45n92
Venturi, Franco 63
Villani, Luisa 27n46, 192n74
Violinista [Violinist], pseudonym of Scoccimarro, Mauro 175, 175n50
Visentini, Bruno 20n31, 92
Vivanti, Giulio 115
Voltaire, pseudonym of François-Marie Arouet 106

Wassermann, Jacob 131
Watts, Ronald 52n108

Zanzi 92
Zucca, Fabio 12n7, 29n55

www.ingramcontent.com/pod-product-compliance
Lightning Source LLC
Chambersburg PA
CBHW020929090426
42736CB00010B/1083